CHRIST AND THE POWERS OF DARKNESS

J. GODFREY RAUPERT

Martino Publishing
Mansfield Centre, CT
2015

Martino Publishing
P.O. Box 373,
Mansfield Centre, CT 06250 USA

ISBN 978-1-61427-836-8

© *2015 Martino Publishing*

Cover design by T. Matarazzo

Printed in the United States of America On 100% Acid-Free Paper

CHRIST AND THE POWERS OF DARKNESS

J. GODFREY RAUPERT

HERDER
St. Louis
1914

Nihil Obstat:
Edwardus Myers,
Censor Deputatus

Imprimatur:
Edmundus Canonicus Surmont,
Vicarius Generalis

Westmonasterii,
Die 13 Julii, 1914

CONTENTS.

INTRODUCTORY.

The argument of this work is based upon the following statement of our Lord Jesus Christ, recorded in the Gospel of St. Matthew (xii., 28).

" . . . if I, by the Spirit of God, cast out devils then is the Kingdom of God come upon you."

It is clear from this statement that our Lord claimed His manifest power over the unclean and evil spirits, possessing and tormenting mankind, to be one of the many proofs of the divinely authoritative character of His mission. If these spirits were really subject unto Him, the only possible inference was that He possessed a power and an authority, distinct from and unlike any other power and authority, possessed by created beings.

The fact of the existence and operation of this power was admitted by His enemies and opponents, the Jews, in whose interest it was to deny and disprove it. Unable to do this, they sought to evade the inference by ascribing the power to Beelzebub, the chief and prince of the devils.

But our Lord's reasoning to the effect that this would be the presenting to the world of a house divided against itself, and of satan casting out satan, appealed to the judgment of His hearers, and the constant and beneficent display of this power brought both Jews and Gentiles to His feet. In the light of the New Testament Records our Lord's life on earth has been rightly described as a ceaseless conflict with the devil— as a struggle of the powers of light and truth with the powers of darkness and error. What Christ had come for was " to destroy the works of the devil."* So clear is this fact from the Sacred Writings that a rationalising theologian like Harnack is constrained to write :

" In order to estimate the significance of exorcism for primitive Christianity, one must remember that, according to the belief of Christians, the Son of God came into the world to combat satan and his kingdom."

* I. St. John iii., 8.

8

" The evangelists, especially Luke, have depicted the life of Jesus from the Temptation onwards as an uninterrupted conflict with the devil : what He came for was to destroy the works of the devil."*

A scientific student of the subject who has also carefully weighed all that the Gospels and Epistles have to say about the matter and that the early history of Christianity records, sums up his conclusions in the following words :—

" The Incarnation initiated the establishment of the Kingdom of Heaven upon earth. That determined a counter-movement among the powers of darkness. Genuine demonic possession was one of its manifestations."†

Further reflection makes it clear that the entire scheme of the Incarnation and of the Redemption of man through Christ implies and presupposes the existence of the devil and his angels, and the constant action upon man of a hostile spirit-world.

*The Expansion of Christianity in the First Three Centuries.
†W. Menzies Alexander, M.A., M..D

CHRIST AND THE POWERS OF DARKNESS

The supernatural truths of Christianity lose their force and consistency when this pre-supposition is denied and ignored and when purely natural forces are believed to be responsible for the sins and the misery of the world.

So fully is this recognised by thinkers hostile to Christianity that Voltaire, the French infidel, was led to make the following statement :

" Sathan ! c'est le Christianism tout entier ; pas de Sathan, pas de Sauveur. (satan ! this is Christianity entire; no satan, no Saviour.)

Bayle, another uncompromising opponent of Historical Christianity, declared :

" Prove to unbelievers the existence of evil spirits, and you will, by that alone, force them to concede all your dogmas."*

Monticelli, quoted by Perrone†, commenting upon this remark of Voltaire's, develops the thought in the following form :

*The Christian Religion. A series of articles from the North American Review. New York, 1882, p. 86.
†De Virtute Religionis, p. 298.

" The remark is a compendium of the entire theology of Redemption. . . . For if there is no satan, or if he takes no interest (azione) in the world, then it is also not true what St. John says that Christ came to destroy the works of satan (ut dissolvat opera diaboli) (I. St. John iii. 8). Hence (if there is) no satan, (there is also) no fall of man; (if there is) no fall of man, (there is) no Redemption, no Redeemer; (if there is) no Redeemer, (there is) no Christianity, (there is) no religion; (if there is) no religion, (there is) no God.

And, indeed, it was by commencing to joke about (scherzar sopra) satan, by denying satan, that the philosophers of the last century and of the present have terminated by joking about God, by denying God. Hence one comprehends the interest satan and his satellites have in being unknown and denied. (Si comprende adunque l'interresse che ha satana e i suoi satelliti perchè si disconosca e si neghi.)"

It is to be observed that in the records of the Sacred Scriptures physical disease is clearly distinguished from the operations of evil spirits, our Lord being reported to have healed the former as well as to have delivered those afflicted by the latter. The modern contention, therefore, that ordinary bodily disease was, in that age, confounded with possession by evil spirits falls to the ground.

In some instances there is conclusive evidence that the bodily disease was really intimately connected with the operation of evil spirits, the disease disappearing at the pronouncement of Christ's exorcising words. In many instances the spirits were made to confess what they were.

Already during His life and work on earth our Lord conveyed to His twelve Apostles the same power over the evil spirits which He Himself possessed. By virtue of this transmitted power of His they were commissioned and enabled to do what He had done.

And it is evident from the Sacred Scriptures that the twelve successfully exercised this power and that, by virtue of this exercise, the world believed in them and in their mission and consequently in the divinity of Christ.

The belief in the personal devil and his angels, therefore, and in the power of the priest, ordained and consecrated by Christ to cast them out, formed one of the articles of the creed of the earliest Church. It would seem to have been the element in the Christian teaching which proved most instrumental in furthering the spread of Christianity among the pagan nations.

After the descent of the Holy Ghost on the day of Pentecost which, as we can scarcely doubt, still further deepened and strengthened this power already possessed by the twelve, they forthwith began to exercise it, for the book of the Acts of the Apostles gives record of their successful casting out of evil spirits in the name of Christ.

The twelve again transmitted their power to those who came after them and whom they ordained and consecrated in Christ's name. They too cast out devils, and they too appealed to this manifest fact as evidence that both their message and their mission were divine.

13

We have, it should be borne in mind, not a single statement on the part of the heathen urbelievers of those days from which it can be inferred that they doubted the existence of evil spirits and the power of the Church over them, and that they held this belief to be an error and a delusion.

In all the succeeding centuries the Church has unceasingly taught that she possesses this power over the spirits of darkness, and there is abundant and trustworthy evidence to show that she has, in numerous instances, successfully exercised it. This teaching is embodied in all her formularies, and the priests she ordains to minister at her altars to-day are also ordained exorcists.

One of the greatest errors of our own time, therefore, is the common assumption that evil spirits do not exist, or that if they exist, they no longer obsess and torment man.

This assumption, which is wholly without foundation, must be ascribed to the work of modern rationalising critics of the New

Testament, and to the false reasonings of some scientific men who have no very accurate knowledge of the subject. In some measure, no doubt, it is also due to the circumstance that the evil spirits are apt to change the *mode* of their operation, adapting it to the thoughts and tendencies of a particular time and age and a particular people.

The evidence, recently derived from careful and experimental research, by men of real scientific eminence and of different nationality, has made it abundantly clear that a spirit-world exists, and that it is, under many disguises and in a variety of forms, seeking intercourse with the sense-world.

A positively evil element has been shown to be constantly displaying itself in connection with these researches, and the phenomena of obsession and possession are being increasingly admitted to be of frequent occurrence. The helplessness of science, however, with respect to these preternatural phenomena is daily becoming more manifest.

15

The power of Christ, on the other hand, over the spirits of darkness, working in His Church and manifesting itself in His true Sacraments and through the agency of His validly ordained and commissioned instruments, cannot be doubted by those who have real experience of the matter.

But if this be so, if the spirits of evil are really subject unto Him, we have in the present age too, conclusive and even experimental evidence that Christ and His Church are divine. We are bound, in this age, too, to recognise the full significance of those words:

" . . . if I, by the Spirit of God, cast out devils then is the kingdom of God come upon you."

Some counsels and suggestions are added with a view to safeguarding and helping those who may be consciously or unconsciously striving with the powers of darkness. These counsels are based upon a wide and many-sided practical experience and upon inferences drawn from actual occurrences which have come to the author's knowledge in the course of his researches.

I.

" The New Testament," writes Dr. Cunningham Geikie*, " leaves no doubt of the belief in the reality of these demoniacal possessions on the part of Jesus and the Evangelists. . . . Modern criticism has sought to attribute the phenomena associated with possession, to physical and mental causes only, but the fact that disease takes the same forms from apparently natural causes as it assumed from the action of evil spirits, leaves the possibility of its being associated with their presence in the cases recorded in the New Testament, wholly untouched. There are more things in heaven and on earth than are dreamed of in our philosophy."

The Testimony of the New Testament.

II.

From the New Testament we gather the following :

ST. MATTHEW IV. I-II.

(See also St. Luke iv. I-13).

1. Then Jesus was led by the spirit into the desert, to be tempted by the devil.

*The Life and Words of Christ. New York, 1885.

17

2

2. And when He had fasted forty days and forty nights, afterwards he was hungry.

3. And the tempter coming said to him : If thou be the Son of God, command that these stones be made bread.

4. Who answered and said : It is written, Not in bread alone doth man live, but in every word that proceedeth from the mouth of God.

5. Then the devil took him up into the holy city, and set him upon the pinnacle of the temple.

6. And said to him : If thou be the Son of God, cast thyself down, for it is written : That he hath given his Angels charge over thee, and in their hands they shall bear thee up, lest perhaps thou dash thy foot against a stone.

7. Jesus said to him, It is written again : Thou shalt not tempt the Lord thy God.

8. Again the devil took him up into a very high mountain : and showed him all the kingdoms of the world, and the glory of them.

9. And said to him : All these will I give thee, if falling down thou wilt adore me.

10. Then Jesus saith to him: Begone, Satan: for it is written: The Lord thy God shalt thou adore, and him only shalt thou serve.

11. Then the devil left him: and behold Angels came and ministered to him.

ST. MATTHEW IV. 24.

24. And his fame went throughout all Syria, and they presented to him all sick people that were taken with divers diseases and torments, *and such as were possessed by devils* and lunatics, and those that had the palsy, and he cured them.

25. And much people followed him from Galilee, and from Decapolis, and from Jerusalem, and from Judea, and from beyond the Jordan.

ST. MATTHEW VIII., 16.

16. And when evening was come, they brought to him many that were possessed with devils: *and he cast out the spirits with his word*: and all that were sick he healed.

St. Matthew viii., 28, etc.

28. And when he was come on the other side of the water, into the country of the Gerasens, *there met him two that were possessed with devils,* coming out of the sepulchres, exceeding fierce, so that none could pass by that way.

29. And behold they cried out, saying : What have we to do with thee, Jesus Son of God ? Art thou come hither to torment us before the time ?

St. Matthew ix., 33.

32. And when they were gone out, behold they brought him a dumb man, possessed with a devil.

33. And *after the devil was cast out, the dumb man spoke,* and the multitudes wondered, saying, Never was the like seen in Israel.

34. But the Pharisees said, By the prince of devils he casteth out devils.

CHRIST AND THE POWERS OF DARKNESS

ST. MATTHEW X., 1.

And having called his twelve disciples together, *he gave them power over unclean spirits, to cast them out,* and to heal all manner of diseases, and all manner of infirmities.

ST. MATTHEW X., 7.

7. And going, preach, saying: The kingdom of heaven is at hand.

8. Heal the sick, raise the dead, cleanse the lepers, *cast out devils;* freely have you received, freely give.

ST. MATTHEW XII., 22, etc.

22. *Then was offered to him one possessed with a devil, blind and dumb; and he healed him, so that he spoke and saw.*

23. *And all the multitudes were amazed,* and said: is not this the son of David?

24. But the Pharisees hearing it, said: This man casteth not out devils, but by Beelzebub the prince of the devils.

25. And Jesus knowing their thoughts, said to them : Every kingdom divided against itself shall be made desolate : and every city or house divided against itself shall not stand.

26. And if satan cast out satan, he is divided against himself; how then shall his kingdom stand ?

27. And if I by Beelzebub cast out devils, by whom do your children cast them out ? Therefore they shall be your judges.

28. But *if I by the Spirit of God cast out devils, then is the kingdom of God come upon you.*

29. Or how can any one enter into the house of the strong, and rifle his goods, unless he first bind the strong ? and then he will rifle his house.

30. He that is not with me, is against me : and he that gathereth not with me, scattereth.

St. Matthew xii., 43.

43. And when an unclean spirit is gone out of a man he walketh through dry places seeking rest, and findeth none.

22

44. Then he saith: I will return into my house from whence I came out. And coming he findeth it empty, swept, and garnished.

45. Then he goeth, and taketh with him seven other spirits more wicked than himself, and they enter in and dwell there: and the last state of that man is made worse than the first. So shall it be also to this wicked generation.

St. Matthew XIII., 25.

25. But while men were asleep, his enemy came and oversowed cockle among the wheat, and went his way.

St. Matthew XIII., 39.

39. *And the enemy that sowed them, is the devil.*

St. Matthew XV., 22.

22. And behold a woman of Canaan who came out of those coasts, crying out, said to him: Have mercy on me, O Lord, thou son of David: my daughter is grievously troubled by a devil.

23. Who answered her not a word, And his disciples came and besought him, saying: Send her away, for she crieth after us:

24. And he answering, said: I was not sent but to the sheep that are lost of the house of Israel.

25. But she came and adored him, saying: Lord, help me.

26. Who answering, said: It is not good to take the bread of the children, and to cast it to the dogs.

27. But she said: Yea, Lord: for the whelps also eat of the crumbs that fall from the table of their masters.

28. Then Jesus answering, said to her: O woman, great is thy faith: be it done to thee as thou wilt: and *her daughter was cured from that hour.*

St. Matthew xvii., 14.

14. And when he was come to the multitude there came to him a man falling down on his knees before him, saying: Lord, have pity on my son, for he is a lunatic, and suffereth

much : for he falleth often into the fire, and often into the water.

15. And I brought him to thy disciples, and they could not cure him.

16. Then Jesus answered and said : O unbelieving and perverse generation, how long shall I be with you ? How long shall I suffer you ? Bring him hither to me.

17. *And Jesus rebuked him, and the devil went 'out of him, and the child was cured from that hour.*

18. Then came the disciples to Jesus secretly, and said : Why could not we cast him out ?

19. Jesus said to them : Because of your unbelief. For, amen, I say to you, if you have faith as a grain of mustard-seed, you shall say to this mountain, Remove from hence hither, and it shall remove : and nothing shall be impossible to you.

20. But this kind is not cast out but by prayer and fasting.

ST. MARK III., 11.

11. *And the unclean spirits, when they saw him, fell down before him: and they cried, saying:*

12. *Thou art the Son of God. And he strictly charged them that they should not make him known.*

ST. MARK VI., 17.

17. And these signs shall follow them that believe: *In my name they shall cast out devils :* etc.

ST. LUKE X., 17.

17. *And the seventy-two returned with joy, saying: Lord, the devils also are subject to us in thy name.*

18. And he said to them: I saw satan like lightning falling from heaven.

19. Behold, I have given you power to tread upon serpents and scorpions, and upon all the power of the enemy, and nothing shall hurt you.

20. But yet rejoice not in this that spirits are subject unto you : but rejoice in this, that your names are written in heaven.

St. Luke XII., 3.

3. *And satan entered into Judas* who was surnamed Iscariot, one of the twelve.

4. And he went and discoursed with the chief priests and the magistrates, how he might betray him to them.

St. Luke XXII., 52.

52. And Jesus said to the chief priests, and magistrates of the temple, and the ancients that were come unto him : Are you come out, as it were against a thief, with swords and clubs ?

53. When I was daily with you in the temple you did not stretch forth your hands against me; but *this is your hour, and the power of darkness.*

54. And apprehending him, they led him to the high-priest's house.

27

St. John VIII., 42.

42. Jesus therefore said to them : If God were your father, you would indeed love me. For from God I proceeded, and came : for I came not of myself, but he sent me.

43. Why do you not know my speech? Because you cannot hear my word.

44. *You are of your father the devil,* and the desires of your father you will do. He was a murderer from the beginning, and he stood not in the truth. When he speaketh a lie, he speaketh of his own : for he is a liar, and the father thereof.

45. But if I say the truth, you believe me not.

Acts v., 1.

But a certain man named Ananias, with Saphira his wife, sold a piece of land.

2. And by fraud kept back part of the price of the land, his wife being privy thereunto; and bringing a certain part of it, laid it at the feet of the apostles.

3. But *Peter said* : *Ananias, why hath satan tempted thy heart,* that thou shouldst lie to the Holy Ghost, and by fraud keep part of the price of the land ?

4. Whilst it remained, did it not remain to thee ? And after it was sold, was it not in thy power ? **Why hast thou conceived this thing in thine heart? Thou hast not lied to men, but to God.**

5. And Ananias hearing these words, fell down, and gave up the ghost. And there came great fear upon all that heard it.

ACTS V., 16.

16. And there came also together to Jersualem a multitude out of the neighbouring cities, *bringing* sick persons, and *such as were troubled with unclean spirits; who were all healed.*

ACTS VIII., 6.

6. And the people with one accord were attentive to those things which were said by Philip, hearing, and seeing the miracles which he did.

7. For *many of them who had unclean spirits, crying with a loud voice, went out.*

ACTS VIII., 9.

9. Now there was a certain man named Simon, who before had been a magician in that city, seducing the people of Samaria, giving out that he was some great one:

10. To whom they all gave ear, from the least to the greatest, saying: This man is the power of God, which is called great.

11. And they were attentive to him, because *for a long time he had bewitched them with his magical practices.*

12. But when they had believed Philip preaching of the kingdom of God, in the name of Jesus Christ, they were baptised both men and women.

13. Then Simon himself believed also: and being baptised, he stuck close to Philip. And being astonished, wondered to see the signs and exceeding great miracles which were done.

ACTS XIII., 6.

6. And when they had gone through the whole island as far as Paphos, *they found a certain man a magician, a false prophet,* a Jew, whose name was Bar-jesu.

7. Who was with the proconsul Sergius Paulus, a prudent man. He, sending for Barnabas and Saul, desired to hear the word of God.

8. But Elymas the magician (for so his name is interpreted) withstood them, seeking to turn away the proconsul from the faith.

9. *Then Saul, otherwise Paul, filled with the Holy Ghost, looking upon him,*

10. *Said : O full of all guile, and of all deceit, child of the devil,* enemy of all justice, thou ceasest not to pervert the right ways of the Lord.

11. And now behold the hand of the Lord is upon thee, and thou shalt be blind, not seeing the sun for a time. And immediately there fell a mist and a darkness upon him, and going about, he sought some one to lead him by the hand.

31

12. Then the proconsul, when he had seen what was done, believed, admiring at the doctrine of the Lord.

ACTS XVI., 16.

16. And it came to pass as we went to prayer, *a certain girl having a pythonical spirit, met us, who brought to her masters much gain by divining.*

17. This same following Paul and us, cried out, saying: These men are the servants of the most high God, who preach unto you the way of salvation.

18. And this she did many days. But *Paul being grieved, turned and said to the spirit: I command thee, in the name of Jesus Christ, to go out from her. And he went out the same hour.*

19. But her masters seeing that the hope of their gain was gone, apprehending Paul and Silas, brought them into the market-place to the rulers.

ACTS XIX., II.

11. *And God wrought by the hand of Paul more than common miracles.*

12. So that even there were brought from his body to the sick handkerchiefs and aprons, and the diseases departed from them, *and the wicked spirits went out of them.*

13. Now some also of the Jewish exorcists, who went about tempted to invoke, over them that had evil spirits, the name of the Lord Jesus, saying : I conjure you by Jesus whom Paul preacheth.

14. And there were certain men, seven sons of Sceva, a Jew, a chief priest, that did this.

15. But the wicked spirit answering, said to them : Jesus I know, and Paul I know : but who are you ?

16. And the man in whom the wicked spirit was, leaping upon them and mastering them both, prevailed against them, so that they fled out of that house naked and wounded.

17. And this became known to all the Jews and the Gentiles that dwelt at Ephesus : and

fear fell on them all, and the name of the Lord Jesus was magnified.

18. And many of them that believed came confessing and declaring their deeds.

19. And many of them who had followed curious arts, brought together their books and burnt them before all : and counting the price of them, they found the money to be fifty thousand pieces of silver.

20. So mightily grew the word of God and was confirmed.

II. COR. XI., 13.

13. For such false apostles are deceitful workmen, transforming themselves into the apostles of **Christ.**

14. And no wonder : for *satan himself transformeth himself into an angel of light.*

15. Therefore it is no great thing if his ministers be transformed as the ministers of justice : whose end shall be according to their **works.**

34

EPHES. VI., 10.

10. Finally, brethren, be strengthened in the Lord, and in the might of his power.

11. Put you on the armour of God, that you may be able to stand against the deceits of the devil.

12. For *our wrestling is not against flesh and blood : but against principalities and powers, against the rulers of the world of this darkness, against the spirits of wickedness in the high places.*

13. Therefore take unto you the armour of God, that you may be able to resist in the evil day, and to stand in all things perfect.

14. Stand therefore, having your loins girt about with truth, and having on the breast-plate of justice.

15. And your feet shod with the preparation of the gospel of peace :

16. In all things taking the shield of faith, wherewith you may be able to extinguish all the fiery darts of the most wicked one.

35

I. TIM. IV., I.

Now the Spirit manifestly saith, that *in the last times some shall depart from the faith, giving heed to spirits of error, and doctrines of devils,*

2. Speaking lies in hypocrisy, and having their conscience seared,

3. Forbidding to marry, to abstain from meats, which God hath created to be received with thanksgiving by the faithful, and by them that have known the truth.

II. TIM. II., 24.

24. But the servant of the Lord must not wrangle : but be mild towards all men, apt to teach, patient,

25. With modesty admonishing them that resist the truth : if peradventure God may give them repentance to know the truth,

26. *And they may recover themselves from the snares of the devil, by whom they are held captive at his will.*

St. James iv., 7.

7. Be subject therefore to God, but *resist the devil and he will fly from you.*

8. Draw nigh to God, and he will draw nigh to you.

I. St. Peter v. 8.

8. *Be sober and watch: because your adversary the devil, as a roaring lion, goeth about seeking whom he may devour.*

9. Whom resist ye, strong in faith: knowing that the same affliction befalls your brethren who are in the world.

10. But the God of all grace, who hath called us unto His eternal glory in Christ Jesus, after you have suffered a little, will Himself perfect you, and confirm you, and establish you.

11. To Him be glory and empire for ever and ever. Amen.

I. St. John iii., 7.

7. Little children, let no man deceive you. He that doeth justice, is just: even as he is just.

8. He that committeth sin is of the devil: for the devil sinneth from the beginning. For this purpose the Son of God appeared that he might destroy the works of the devil.

9. Whosoever is born of God, committeth not sin : for his seed abideth in him, and he cannot sin, because he is born of God.

10. In this the children of God are manifest, and the children of the devil. Whosoever is not just, is not of God, nor he that loveth not his brother.

APOC. XII., 9.

9. And that great dragon was cast out, that old serpent, who is called the devil and satan, who seduceth the whole world : and he was cast unto the earth, and his angels were thrown down with him.

10. And I heard a loud voice in heaven saying : Now is come salvation, and strength, and the kingdom of our God, and the power of his Christ : because the accuser of our brethren is cast forth, who accused them before our God day and night.

38

11. And they overcame him by the blood of the Lamb, and by the word of the testimony, and they loved not their lives unto death.

SEE ALSO I. ST. JOHN IV., 1-3.

III.

From the writings of the earliest Christian Fathers and Philosophers it is abundantly clear that they thoroughly believed evil spirits to be at the bottom of pagan idolatry and to be the inspirers of the minds of the opponents of Christianity. They pointed to the manifest power of the Church over these evil spirits as incontrovertible evidence of the truth of the Incarnation and of the divinity of Jesus Christ.

The Testimony of the earliest Christian writers.

IV.

ST. JUSTIN, the philosopher, who became a Christian in 135 and was martyred in 166, writes in his second " Apology " (c. vi.) that the Son of God assumed human nature " for the salvation of believing mankind and the ruin of demons." And, addressing the pagan Romans, he says :

39

" Even now you can learn this from what happens before your own eyes. For many of ours (namely of the Christians) have healed and still do heal by making powerless and casting out the devils by which such persons are possessed, a great number of possessed persons, in the whole world and in your city here (Rome) by exorcisms in the name of Jesus Christ, crucified under Pontius Pilate; after these (possessed persons) could not be healed by all . . . . conjurors and magicians and medicine men."

Again he writes* :

" For nothing else is it that the demons (or the devils) strive after than to draw men away from God the Creator and from Christ His Only Begotten."

In his dialogue with the Jew Tryphon," St. Justin remarks :

" Any demon, adjured by the name of this Son of God (Jesus) will be vanquished. . . . But if (demons were conjured) by any name of those who were either kings, or just ones, or prophets, or patriarchs among you (Jews) no demon would be overcome."

*1st Apology, 58.

40

V.

MINUTIUS FELIX, a learned Roman lawyer and, after his conversion to Christianity, one of the earliest Latin writers, says the following : *

" All this is known to the majority of you (pagans), that the demons confess of themselves, as they are driven by us (Christians) out of bodies by means of the torments of exorcisms (verborum) and by the fires of prayers. Saturnus himself, and Serapis, and Jupiter, and all the demons you (pagans) worship, overcome by pain, proclaim what they are; and certainly they do not lie to their own disgrace, especially when some of you (pagans) are present. As they confess themselves to be demons, believe them; for, adjured by the true and only God, they, against their will, shudder in the possessed bodies and either leave suddenly or vanish gradually, in proportion as the faith of the patient helps, or the grace of the exorcising assists (gratia curantis aspirat).

*H. Hurter, S.J. *Sanctorum Patrum Opuscula Selecta.* Vol. 15, pp. 79-80.

VI.

St. Irenaeus, the disciple of St. Polycarp, who died a martyr in 202, writes as follows* :

" Some of them (the disciples of Jesus Christ) most certainly and truly cast out devils, so that very often those themselves who were freed from the evil spirits turn believers."

VII.

St. Theophilus, who was Bishop of Antioch in the 2nd Century, writes in his treatise addressed to Autolycus : †

" The poets, namely Homer and Hesiod, inspired by the muses, as is said, spoke according to imagination and delusion, inspired, not by a pure but by a deceitful spirit. This is clearly proved by the fact that persons agitated by a demon are, up to the present time, sometimes exorcised in the name of the true God, and that then the deceitful spirits themselves confess to be demons that once were operating in those poets."

*Against Heresies, ii., 32, 4.
†ii., ch. 8.

VIII.

ST. CYPRIAN, Bishop of Carthage in the 3rd Century, has striking references in his writings to the power which the Christians of his day exercised over possessing spirits. In his work addressed to the pagan philosopher Demetrian* he says:

" O, if thou would'st hear and see them (the demons) when they are adjured by us, and tormented with spiritual scourges, and cast out of the obsessed bodies by means of the tortures of exorcism (verborum); when lamenting and groaning with human voice, and feeling through divine power, the scourges and stripes, they confess the coming judgment! Come and learn from observation that we speak the truth. . . . Thou wilt see those standing bound and trembling as captives under our hand, on whom you look and whom you worship as lords (gods)."

In another of his works† St. Cyprian writes:

" Adjured by the true God they (the demons) give way to us immediately and

*H. Hurter, S.J.   Vol. 1, p. 51.
†De Idolorum Vanitate.

43

confess, and they are compelled to quit the bodies which they possessed. You can observe how, at our word and prayer, they are stricken with scourges of hidden (divine) majesty, (how they are) burned by fire, (how they are) tormented by the continually increasing pains, how they whine, groan, beg, how they confess whence they came and when they will depart even in the presence of their worshippers."

Again he writes :*

" These spirits are hidden beneath consecrated statues and images; they inspire with their breath the breast of the seers; they enliven the fibres of the entrails (of sacrificed animals); they govern the flight of the birds; they direct the lots; they cause oracles; they always surround falsehood with truth; they disturb life; they disquiet sleep; entering secretly into the bodies, these spirits also frighten the soul, dislocate members (of the body), ruin health; (and) cause diseases, to compel people to worship them; so that they

*De Idolorum Vanitate, 7.

may seem to have cured, when, satisfied by the smoke of the altars and the burned animal sacrifices, they let free again what they had entangled.''

IX.

The clear discernment of these early Christians is perhaps most forcibly expressed in the following striking words of this saintly Bishop and martyr :

" He (the devil with his evil fellow-spirits) has made heresies and schisms, wherewith to subvert faith, to corrupt truth, and to rend unity. . . . He snatches men from the Church itself, and while they think themselves come to light . . . he secretly gathers fresh shadows upon them; so that standing neither with the Gospel of Christ, nor with His ordinances, nor with His law, they call themselves Christians, walking among darkness and thinking they have light, while the foe flatters and misleads, transforming himself, according to the word of the Apostle, into an angel of light, and garbs his ministers as ministers of righteousness.''

45

X.

TERTULLIAN, in his famous Apology*
addressed to the Roman rulers, writes respecting
the demons worshipped by the pagans that their
work is the overthrow and destruction of mankind. To this end, he says, they inflict sick-
nesses and certain painful ills of the body as well
as sudden, extraordinary, and violent ' excesses '
of the soul. He points out that their apparently
beneficent operation in the care of ailments is
deceptive, since they first cause the sickness and
by then ceasing to inflict injury and by prescrib-
ing new remedies they give to their apparent
cure the semblance of a miracle.

XI.

At another place in his work Tertullian
emphasizes the fact that Christians can compel
the demons, in the name of Jesus, to confess the
truth. He says:

" Being commanded by any Christian to
speak, such a spirit will just as truly confess
to be a devil, as he elsewhere falsely pretends
to be a god."

*Chapter 22.

And it is surely worthy of note that about a thousand years before St. Thomas Aquinas, and nearly 2,000 years before the rise of Modern Spiritism, Tertullian declared that

"magicians, with the help of devils, cause apparitions and disgrace the souls of the dead" (phantasmata edunt et jam defunctorum infamant animas.)*.

He expresses the same conviction in his book *De Anima*†, and adds that this fraud of the evil spirit—who hides himself behind deceased persons (fallacia Spiritus nequam sub personis defunctorum delitescentis) is occasionally exposed during the exorcisms, when such a spirit at first claims to be one of the parents of the possessed; then some gladiator or matadore (bestiarius); and then again, some god.

"But finally," Tertullian continues, "this demon, after having tried to delude those present, overcome by the persistence of divine grace, confesses reluctantly who he is (Et tamen ille daemon, postquam circumstantes

Apologeticum, c. p. 23.
†Chapter 57.

47

circumvenire tentavit, instantia divinae gratiae victus, id quod in vero est invitus confitetur.'')

XII.

It is a well-attested fact that the oracle of Apollo at Daphne near Antioch ceased to answer after the relics of the martyr St. Babylas (A.D. 251) had been transferred to that place. The oracle gave answers again when Julian the apostate had removed these relics.*

XIII.

It is also asserted† that the Emperor Diocletian, who for a period of eighteen years had treated the Christians with singular favour, allowing them perfect freedom of worship and even appointing them to offices in his own court, suddenly initiated a persecution lasting ten years and surpassing in cruelty all that had gone before it. He was induced to change his mind upon being informed that the oracle of Apollo declared itself unable to utter true predictions on

* Perrone : *De Virtute Religionis,* p. 327.
†*Eusebius* : *Vita Constantinii,* lib., ii·

account of the presence of the just men on earth.
Upon enquiry he was told by one of the pagan
priests that the just men were the Christians.

XIV.

LACTANTIUS, writing in the 4th Century*,
remarks :

" The demons fear the just, that is the
worshippers of God; when adjured in His
name they (the demons) leave the bodies (of
the possessed); struck by the exorcisms
(verbis) as with scourges, they not only confess to be demons, but also give those as their
names that are adored in the temples; and this
they do often in the presence of their
worshippers. . . . They often exclaim
crying loudly, that they are being scourged
and burned, and that they will presently
leave; such is the power of the knowledge and
justice of God."

Lanctantius also speaks of the power of the
Christians over the evil spirits as one of the
causes of the rapid spread of Christianity.

Institutionum Divinarum Libri, vii.

XV.

The great St. Athanasius, Archbishop of Alexandria, also writing in the 4th Century,* says :

" Formerly the demons deceived men with deceptive apparitions . . . and by means of them confounded the foolish. But now, after the divine appearance of the Word has taken place, this deception has come to an end. For man, by using only the sign of the cross, dispels their fraud. . . . Let anyone who desires to convince himself of this, come, and, in the midst of the illusions of the demons, the fraud of the oracles, and the juggleries of witchcraft, make use of the sign of the cross, and only pronounce the name of Christ, and he will see how the demons will take to flight, how the oracles grow dumb, and how every magic and witchcraft become powerless."

Again St. Athanasius writes :†

" When all the frenzy of the demons recedes and flies before His name, it is certainly plain

†*The Incarnation of the Word of God* Ch. 47-55.
*Ibid. Ch. 47-55.

50

. . . that Christ is our Lord and Redeemer, and not as they (the pagans) think a demoniacal power." . . . If He were but a man, how could only one man surpass all their gods (of the pagans) in power and convince them by His power that they were nothing (no gods). But if they (the pagans) call Him (Christ) a sorcerer, how is it possible that by one sorcerer all sorceries have been destroyed and not rather confirmed? For if He had overcome (but some) sorcerers or only one, they (the pagans) might righly believe that by some higher power he excelled the others in the art. But since His Cross has been victorious over every kind of sorcery and even its name, it is certainly evident that the Redeemer is no sorcerer, before Whom, as before their Lord, even the demons invoked by . . . sorcerers take to flight."

In his " Life of St. Antony the Anchorite," St. Athanasius tells us that the latter was one night attacked by a number of evil spirits and so badly maltreated that he lay for a long time speechless on the ground.

XVI.

Students of HERODOTUS will remember his account of how King Crœsus of Lydia once tested the genuineness of the oracle at Delphi. He sent messengers to enquire of the oracle what the king was doing on the hundredth day after his departure from Sardis. On the hundredth day he cut up a tortoise and a lamb and boiled them in a brazen cauldron with a cover of brass upon it. The message of the Pythia was as follows :—

"I know the number of the sands and the measure of the sea; I understand the dumb and hear him that does not speak; the savour of the hard-shelled tortoise boiled in brass with the flesh of lamb strikes on my senses; brass is laid beneath it and brass is put over it."

Compare this with the incident recorded in the book of the Acts of the Apostles (xvi,. 16). St. Paul, in speaking of the spirit cast out of a girl by him as a "Pythonic spirit," is evidently alluding to the Pythia of Delphi.

XVII.

ST. AUGUSTINE, writing in the 5th Century*, relates of a certain Tribunitius Hesperius, living at his time, that his household and animals were greatly annoyed by evil spirits. One of the priests of the diocese over which St. Augustine presided, went to the place, offered up the Holy Sacrifice of Mass (sacrificium corporis Christi) and prayed earnestly that the annoyance might cease. It ceased at once.

XVIII.

In a passage quoted by St. Thomas Aquinas, St. Augustine also says of the demons that they sometimes learn with the greatest ease (tota facilitate) the dispositions of man, not only such as are expressed by word, but also such as are conceived in thought, when certain signs are thereby expressed on the bodily organism of the soul.

XIX.

ST. THOMAS himself writes† :

"Often demons simulate to be the souls of departed, to confirm heathens who believed this, in their error."

*De Civitate Dei, Lib. 22, cap. 8, n. 7.
†Summa Theologica 1, 89, 8 : 117, 4.

53

XX.

It would, of course, be utterly impossible to present in a work of this kind even part of the evidence for the reality of preternatural agencies and phenomena, and of the power of the Church with regard to them, of which we have such abundant record in the history of the middle ages. Works, specifically dealing with the subject, must be consulted for this purpose. The *honest* and *unprejudiced* student of the subject cannot entertain any doubt that, under the name of witchcraft, and in a somewhat changed form, the same hostile spirit-agency continued its operations throughout these centuries. This fact would have to be recognised even though much that occurred in those days may reasonably be ascribed to self-delusion and to morbid states of the nervous system then very little understood. The evidence on this point is far too strong to be resisted. Many of the phenomena then observed and recorded, moreover, are identical in their character with those observed in the early Christian Centuries and in our own day. I must here content myself with stating what so cautious and sceptical an

54

historian as W. E. H. Lecky has to say on the subject. He writes:

" Those who lived when the evidences of witchcraft existed in profusion and attracted the attention of all classes and of all grades of intellect, must surely have been as competent judges as ourselves, if the question was merely a question of evidence."*

XXI.

One of the most famous and well-attested cases of possession by an evil spirit is that of Nicola Aubry, a young French woman of 16 years of age, who lived about 1565 in the reign of Charles IX. A full account of this case is given by Joseph von Goerres in his "Christliche Mystik." The spirit, who at first claimed to be her grandfather and requested prayers and masses for the repose of his soul, turned out to be an evil spirit and, from some unknown cause, took possession of the girl. When the attacks came on 15 strong persons barely succeeded in holding her. The spirit possessing her understood languages

*History of the Rise and Influence of the Spirit of Rationalism in Europe. Vol. i. pp. 28-29.

which Nicola had never learned. She disclosed the state of conscience of persons assisting at the exorcisms, and things happening at the moment in distant places. It is stated that sometimes 10-12,000 persons, amongst whom were the Papal Nuncio and delegates of Parliament and of the University of Paris, were witnesses of the phenomena.

XXII.

In another case related by Goerres* two Doctors of the Sorbonne addressed the possessed in Hebrew, Greek, and Latin. She answered the questions put in these languages in French, even pointing out a mistake in Greek which one of the Doctors had made, and, moreover, revealed the most secret thoughts of some of those present.

XXIII.

It may here be stated that it is not at all difficult to distinguish the phenomenon of obsession or possession from insanity or nervous

*That of a lady of Nancy named Rainfeing. (1619).

disorder. In the latter case the person affected lives in an imaginary world; he talks of things which he thinks he sees or hears but which have no objective existence. In the former case a knowledge is displayed which investigation often proves to be accurate and which could not have reached the mind in a normal manner. Or a description is given of events occurring at a distance which are found to be correct. There is, in some instances, the further evidence of the intelligent use of a language or of languages never normally acquired.

And a faulty pronunciation does not by any means affect this argument in favour of the action of an independent agency. Goerres gives a case in which an uneducated woman attempted to speak Greek, but made some terrible mistakes in pronunciation. The spirit possessing the woman declared that he was aware of the mistake but that this was the fault of the over-awkward woman, " whose tongue was so badly adapted to that language that he could only with difficulty speak any foreign dialect with it.*

*Mystik, Vol. IV., div. 1, page 252.

XXIV.

Goerres speaks of the disgusting stench which sometimes emanates from possessed persons and which fills the air and adheres to their clothes. He observes that this is the reverse of the delightful " odour of sanctity " noticed in the presence of some saints. (See " British Review," February, 1913, where a similar phenomenon in a case of recent occurrence is recorded.)

XXV.

Experience would also seem to demonstrate that the power of the exorcist over the evil spirit is in proportion to the purity of his conscience and the holiness of his life. In the case of Nicola Aubry, the Bishop performing the exorcism, although going to confession every morning, was on one occasion told by the spirit that he had not confessed. When the Bishop contradicted this statement the spirit replied: " You have confessed, but what kind of a confession was it ? You accused yourself only in a general way. You only said you were angry with your servants and with the Chaplain. Had you told this sin and this (mentioning certain faults) I should not know anything of them, and I could not reproach you as I do now."

These words, it is stated, caused intense astonishment amongst those present.*

XXVI.

For the thoughtful student of this subject there cannot, I think, be the slightest doubt that we have, in many of the phenomena of Modern Occultism and Spiritism, conclusive evidence of the continued operation of the identical powers which have been at work from the earliest days of Christianity and indeed from the beginning of time.

I have already, in my earlier works†, given full consideration to the various arguments which may be urged against this conclusion, both from the standpoint of modern science and from that of non-Catholic theology. I do not propose to re-state them here, but to place before

*History of Nicola Aubry, by Rev. M. Mueller.

†The Dangers of Spiritualism, II. Edit. Modern Spiritism, III. Edit. The Supreme Problem, I. Engl· Edit. Spiritistic Phenomena and Their Interpretation, I. Edit.

the reader some further facts and actual occurrences, of which I have had personal knowledge and experience in the course of my researches. I maintain that it is both right and fair that these occurrences should be studied *in the light of the history of the past,* since it is only by this method that we can hope to arrive at a really accurate judgment respecting them. We cannot surely hope permanently to evade an unwelcome conclusion by the statement of half-truths or by concealing manifest but unpleasant facts under freshly-coined scientific terms. The only difference which, in my opinion, exists between the preternatural phenomena of the past and those of our own day is that the latter present themselves in a somewhat different form from the former, adapting themselves to the scientific spirit of the age and that, while the truer religious instinct of the past seldom failed to discern their true aim and nature, the lax religious temper of the present day not only fails to discern these, but deliberately invites and cultivates such phenomena—with results known only to those who have real experience of the matter.

XXVII.

In confirmation of the truth of this statement I would invite the reader's attention to the following occurrences in our own time. *Phenomena observed in our own time.*

Some years ago the publication of one of my books brought me the acquaintance of an exceptionally thoughtful young man who, although a member of a well-known Anglican family, had become enamoured of Occultism and had ultimately embraced Theosophy. He seemed to have found in that mysterious and complex philosophy the answer to many of those questions which are so strangely agitating the modern mind. He entertained no hostile feelings towards Christianity or the Anglican Church. He had a sort of good-natured toleration for them, believing that they represented useful forms of religious thought which, while helpful to certain orders of mind and perhaps best expressing their highest spiritual conceptions, were wholly impossible and inadequate for others. He looked upon Theosophy as a kind of reconciling factor—a system which could afford to tolerate every form

61

of Religion, since its essential elements and principles were common to all.

But Mr. R— was not merely a reader of occult books. He had also studied and observed the phenomena of Spiritism, the objective reality of which Theosophists admit and acknowledge, although they interpret them in a manner different from Spiritists. And these phenomena had proved of very great interest and attraction to him. He was thus in the habit of attending some of the better class circles which are held in private houses in England, and he had, in the course of time, gained a considerable practical experience in the matter. Fully convinced that the evocation of psychical phenomena involved a certain amount of danger and risk to rash and ill-informed persons of certain temperament, he nevertheless held that, since they tended to throw light upon the mystery of the complex human personality, sensible and level-headed persons were quite justified in indulging in them. He believed that, in many instances, the souls of the dead were concerned with them.

This view, of course, was very diametrically opposed to that which I had advocated in my book, and Mr. R—— came to talk the matter over with me and, if possible, to convince me of the reasonableness of his position. I held very tenaciously to mine, having arrived at it after many years of study and observation; but we met often and discussed the subject from various points of view.

Mr. R—— had a friend—a lady—who, like himself, was an ardent student of psychical phenomena. But she had little sympathy with theosophical teachings. Although rejecting many of the extravagances of the spiritualists, she nevertheless accepted their main position: that the spirits of the dead can and do communicate by means of the séance and the medium. And she was actively engaged in experimental investigation, attending circles in London and cultivating her own " mediumistic " powers. To such an extent indeed was she doing this that Mr. R—— was beginning to get concerned about her, feeling that she might possibly be going too far and be incurring certain well-known dangers. He consequently came to me one day to tell me of his growing uneasiness and to suggest my meeting this lady so that I might incidentally give her a warning.

I arranged to meet my friend Mr. R—— and this lady at dinner one night, and, knowing from experience that by painting the dangers of Spiritism in too striking colours one is apt to overshoot the mark and to leave the impression of being something of a fanatic, I endeavoured to convey a warning in the most delicate and tactful manner possible. I based my argument upon actual facts, telling stories of painful occurrences consequent upon spiritistic experiment. I pointed out the peril of putting too much confidence in the statements and doings of these strange intelligences and the necessity of guarding above all things against the induction of trance and passive-mind states.

Mrs. D—— listened to my stories with every attention and with keen interest: but, while fully conceding that there were dangers in these experiments, she thought that they were not greater than those attending other investigations —that it was possible, moreover, for an observant and level-headed person, to guard against them. Like most Spiritualists she was fully persuaded that, in the matter of these communications, " like attracts like," and that those who were so unfortunate as to draw evil spirits into their sphere had only themselves to thank for it. She was quite convinced that *her* spirits were all right.

My own attitude towards the matter she attributed largely to my religious belief, even though I myself might not be fully aware of this. " Besides this, must we not conclude that the unseen world is peopled by the evil as well as by the good, and must we not consequently *expect* to have these invasions of ' undeveloped ' human souls from time to time ? Our duty surely is to help and instruct them—not to be afraid of them or to leave them in their miserable state of ignorance and aversion to good."

It will be seen that Mrs. D—— had, to a large extent, embraced the popular spiritistic creed, which is apt to be presented in such an attractive and eminently plausible form, and which consequently leads so many thousands astray.

I remember returning home from this dinner party in a somewhat depressed state of mind, for I realised that I had done very little good with my arguments.

65

More than five years passed away, in the course of which I merely heard through my friend from time to time that Mrs. D—— was diligently and enthusiastically continuing her "researches." I then left England on a visit to the Colonies and to America, and was away the better part of two years. On the morning after my return to London the first person of my acquaintance whom I met in the street was my friend Mr. R——. He was in a state of considerable agitation, and seemed delighted at meeting me. He explained that he had been making inquiries as to my whereabouts at the houses of friends and others, but had been told to his disappointment that I was still abroad, and was not expected back in England for some time. He looked upon our meeting in this manner, on the first day of my arrival, as quite a providential occurrence.

In the course of our prolonged conversation Mr. R—— told me the following story. His friend Mrs. D—— had, it seemed, gone deeper and deeper into Spiritism, attending many séances and making every effort to "develop" her own mediumistic powers. In this latter respect she had, after a while, met with considerable success. Quite recently she had, in conjunction with several others, equally interested in the matter, formed a "circle" with a view to obtaining the "higher" phenomena such as the materialisation of spirits, etc. They had succeeded in discovering a powerful medium —a lady who lived some distance from London, and at this lady's house the most successful séances had been taking place for some time. At first everything had gone well, but, after a while, suspicious phenomena had developed, "and now," my friend continued, "there has, I fear, taken place what you predicted more than five years ago. Mrs. D—— is showing all the signs of possession, and I am terribly anxious about her. She knows that there is something radically wrong, and is constantly expressing a desire to see you. She dreads becoming insane, and is under the impression that you alone can help her. I have done what I could by way of hypnotic suggestion, etc., but, to my regret, have not succeeded in bringing her any relief."

We arranged, after some further discussion, to send a telegram to Mrs. D—— telling her of my return to England and of my willingness to help her to the best of my power. We begged her to come up to London without delay, and I promised to remain at home certain hours of the day so that no time might be lost.

Several days passed away, however, without an answer being received to this telegram. Upon enquiry at Mrs. D——'s temporary residence we ascertained that she had, upon receipt of the telegram, left home, and was supposed to have gone to London. But she had not arrived at her London house, nor at the house of any of her London friends where Mr. R—— had made enquiry.

There was nothing more to be done, and, having so much of a practical nature to attend to, the matter after a time passed from my mind.

One morning, several weeks later, while sitting at breakfast, a message to the following effect was sent to me by a neighbouring priest of my acquaintance.

During the preceding night one of his fellow-priests had been called to a house in the neighbourhood at which a lady who had been living there for some weeks had caused great commotion. She had passed into an extraordinary state of nerve-excitement amounting to frenzy, in the course of which she had endeavoured to throw herself out of the window, screaming so loud that the neighbourhood had been disturbed and the police had had to be sent for. Various efforts to calm her had proved unsuccessful, and a doctor who had been called in had urged her speedy removal to an asylum. She was then in the hands of trained nurses who had to watch her night and day.

In her quiet moments, so I was informed, she had continually mentioned my name, begging her attendants to find me and assuring them that I knew the cause of her trouble and that I could help her.

The priest, hearing this and knowing that his fellow-priest was a personal friend of mine, had communicated with him, and his request was to the effect that I would go at once to see this lady.

I left the breakfast table, and hurried to the Presbytery to see the priest who had paid the night-visit, and, in his company, I visited the house. My astonishment was great when, on entering the bedroom, I recognised the poor lady who had so mysteriously disappeared, and whom I had not even remotely connected in my mind with this occurrence.

The nurses were anxious to remain in the room with me, but I managed to get rid of them by pointing out to them that Mrs. D—— had not only fully recognised me, but had become quite quiet and rational in her talk.

When we were alone she took my hand and said: " I need not tell you what has happened. You warned me that night, so many years ago, and I wish I had then taken your warning. But it is too late now. I cannot tell you what I am suffering. These spirits are persecuting me. I can hear their talk, and every now and then one of them takes possession of me. I can see them coming, and when I endeavour to resist, there is the struggle which ends in these fits. Of course my friends think me insane, and purpose sending me to an asylum. But you know what it is, and that I am not insane. You must save me from this terrible fate."

It was an extremely difficult and delicate position for me, and I felt that the matter required full and careful consideration. I therefore advised to the best of my knowledge and power, and promised my visit for the next day. I left the poor lady in a somewhat calmer and certainly more hopeful frame of mind.

There is a peculiar circumstance which I must mention in connection with this my first visit to the house. In order to divert Mrs. D——'s attention I told her something of my journeys and experiences abroad, of places I had visited and interesting people I had met. To my intense amazement she seemed to be well informed, not only with respect to my movements in general, but she supplied details in several instances which could not possibly be known to any person in England. When I asked in my astonishment: "How in the world did you find that out?" she replied very quietly: "Oh! they (the spirits) told me; they kept me well informed!"

After consulting with my clerical friend, a cultured and thoughtful priest, and well acquainted with the intricacies of the modern

71

devilry called Spiritism, we decided to see the medical man who had the case under treatment. Fortunately for poor Mrs. D—— he happened to be a man of enlightened views who was willing to listen to *our* account of the matter and who listened with the keenest interest. Indeed, so little was he the slave of received views on this subject that he admitted that our theory (that of possession) explained the symptoms he had observed much better than his—that of insanity—" provided," he continued, " you do not ask me to believe that these extraordinary spirits are the spirits of the dead."

There were, however, technical difficulties which made it impossible for him, a responsible medical man, to allow this lady to go free and to mix with her fellows. He pointed out to us that the blame would be fixed upon him if any trouble came to her or to others.

I may add, however, that, after a time, Mrs. D—— herself found a way out of this difficulty. She was allowed to return to her home in the charge of a near relative with whom she communicated and who made himself fully responsible.

Some few weeks later, when her health had been somewhat restored, she begged me to meet her at her club in London, and there, in a private room, she told me the following story.

It appears that the " circle " which they had formed at the house mentioned had sat regularly for manifestations—sometimes night after night. " Psychic powers " of remarkable quality had developed very rapidly, and excellent and interesting phenomena had been obtained. The lady, at whose house the meetings took place, proved to be the best medium, but the spirits indicated that her young daughter would prove a better medium still if the sitters would obey instructions and " develop her gifts." They (the spirits) would then be able to produce that most desired of all phenomena, materialisation—that is, they would be able to show themselves in visible and sensible form. Strenuous efforts were then made to obtain this result.

There was, however, one obstructing element in the house. The husband of the mediumistic lady was, it seemed, strongly opposed to these spiritistic practices, against which he never ceased protesting. He was a Nonconformist of the old-fashioned type who held severe and rigid views on the subject. Being an invalid, permanently confined to his bed, it was not in his power to prevent these nightly gatherings. He therefore made it his practice to engage in earnest prayer while they were being held, invoking the divine aid and seeking thereby to frustrate the success of the experiments.

I do not know how far this fact was known to the members of the circle. But it appears that they were informed by the spirits one night that there was an opposing influence in the house in the form of the prayers of the old man, and that if it were not removed, materialisations could not take place. I cannot in this connection state all the astounding circumstances which were communicated to me. Certain it is that the poor invalid swallowed an overdose of his sleeping mixture one night, and died soon after. With his death the difficulty was removed and the desired phenomena occurred.

But a new and quite unexpected development now took place. A spirit, claiming to be the soul of the deceased old man, began to haunt the circle. He was full of malice and revenge, and caused considerable annoyance and disturbance, under which Mrs. D——, it seems, had to suffer most of all. These annoyances, in the course of time, occurred under ordinary conditions when the circle was not sitting, so that the nightly gatherings had to be suspended after a while. But, so far as Mrs. D—— was concerned, the mischief was done, the spirit permanently attached himself to her, haunting and troubling her night and day, and ultimately taking possession of her.

The final phase of this dreadful visitation and punishment has already been told. It very nearly cost this poor lady her reason and her health. It meant for her in any case a shattered constitution, and were it not that her naturally strong will, aided by a revival of her early religious belief, came to her aid I doubt whether a recovery could have taken place. Her end would then have been the asylum, where complete recovery from this form of affliction is but seldom achieved.

I have thus given the mere outline of this sad story, the full details of which would convince any rational person that we are here not concerned with a case of auto-suggestion, or double-personality, or mental dissociation, but with one of genuine possession brought on by spiritistic experiments. My friend Father M——, who knows all the circumstances of the case, is of this opinion, and we have fully and fairly, and from every point of view, considered the arguments which could be urged against it. I may add that Mrs. D—— herself remained convinced of this after her recovery, destructive though it proved to her accepted beliefs and terminating as it did her occult and spiritistic researches.

XXVIII.

The following account has already appeared in print*, but as both the writer and his wife are personal friends of mine, and the former is a well-known scientific authority on psychical research and one who has experienced very great difficulty in accepting any theory of spirit-action, more especially the Catholic one, in connection with these phenomena, I have thought it well to re-print it here:

* *The Supreme Problem.*

76

" You will, I know, be interested in the case I am about to lay before you. A short time ago, if anyone had told me that demoniac possession, such as is spoken of in the Scriptures, now existed, I should have laughed at him. I would do so no longer. I have gone through one of the most extraordinary and one of the most fearful calamities that it is possible for one to experience—at least not I, but my wife. Let me tell you the story.

" Some time ago she became interested in psychic investigation, and tried automatic writing for herself, with the result that, after some patient waiting, she developed into a fluent writer. A ' spirit ' claimed to communicate, and gave a whole life history of himself through the automatic writing. This naturally delighted and interested us immensely. At first, all the communications came through the planchette board; but later on my wife developed writing with a pencil held in the hand; and no sooner had she done so than she began to experience a pain at the back of the brain—at the top of the spine—which increased in intensity as the days went by until

77

it became well-nigh unbearable. Then sleep was interfered with, and her health became affected.

" It was at this stage that the communicating intelligence asserted that he had full command of my wife's body; that he had, in fact, ' obsessed ' her, and that she was no longer a free agent, but subject to his will. We tried hypnotism and mental cures of various kinds without success. We tried all sorts of physical treatment, going on the supposition that we had ordinary insanity to deal with. We tried electricity, baths, diet, fasting, massage, osteopathy, a change of air at the seashore,—all to no benefit. We tried all that doctors could do for her,—likewise a failure. She was pronounced perfectly healthy, physically; no organic or even functional disturbance could be found. More and more she passed under the control and influence of the invading intelligence, and less and less concern had she in the affairs of every-day life. We now became seriously alarmed. I tried to expel the demon by will-power and by commanding him to leave; but all such efforts simply made him worse, and his hold apparently stronger.

"And now a new and a terrible feature developed. Hitherto the impulse had been to *write*,—to write all the time and constantly, with a pen, a pencil, with a finger in the air,—anything, so long as writing was accomplished. But now *voices* resounded in her head—two, three, four voices,—talking to one another, and freely conversing together about her. Some of these voices would praise my wife's conduct, others would blame her. Some would swear and curse, and call her vile names—names she had never heard in her normal state,—while others would try to defend her from these coarser and grosser ones. The voices told her all kinds of things. At first these things were harmless; but as time went by they told her to do things that were far from harmless—suicidal acts, in fact, which she attempted to accomplish. Once they told her to escape at all costs, and she ran out of the house and down the street in her nightgown. Twice they told her to take her own life, and this she attempted to do. She tried to shoot

79

herself; but, fortunately, only inflicted a wound. In other ways they tried to injure her also, and only the best of care prevented a fearful accident on several occasions.

" One curious feature of the case was the fact that my wife realised all the while that these voices were urging her to her own destruction, and yet was unable to resist them. It was as if her own will was entirely in subjection to that of these infernal intelligences. She was quite rational at times, and denied that she was in any way insane; but would argue her case quite rationally, and show you just why it was obsession and not insanity,— as, of course, it is universally conceived to be.

" You may think that this is an ordinary case of insanity, and that we have here no definite proof of ' obsession ' at all; but I can assure you otherwise. There is very good proof that the phenomena are objective and not subjective in their origin. My reason for thinking so is this. During the early stages of my wife's illness, as I may call it, I went to three other well-known mediums in town, and got them to diagnose the case for me, without giving them any clue as to the real state of affairs that existed. They could not possibly have known of her case by hearsay, as it was kept very secret. But each of these three mediums agreed that my wife was obsessed, and described in almost identical terms the kind of evil intelligence that was controlling her; and, furthermore, stated certain things that had happened at our home, which in reality *had* occurred. But better and more conclusive evidence was this: On one occasion the intelligence that claimed to control my wife communicated through another medium, and there asserted that he had done and said certain things at our house which he *had* done and said as a fact. That is, we have here what the Psychical Research Society would call a ' cross reference ' between these two cases,— the same intelligence apparently communicating through both mediums, and stating the same facts through both; also making the claim that he had stated those facts through my wife. Here, then, we have clear evidence of external objective reality,—of an intelligence active and separate from the organism through which it is manifesting. Apart from the internal evidence afforded by the case itself, we have this additional proof that a real intelligence was at work and controlling my wife to do and say the things that she did do and say—against her own will no less than ours.

" Let me say in conclusion that if ever it is proved, by means of such cases as this, that real external intelligences are operative in other cases of what is usually classed as ordinary ' insanity,' it will surely revolutionize medical science and the treatment of the insane. At the present time, the treatment of such cases is almost entirely physiological, and the utter inadequacy of any such treatment was never more clearly shown than in my wife's own case. No! I am persuaded that we have a real case of obsession here,—one similar to many recorded in the Scriptures, and in modern literature, both religious and secular."

XXIX.

Not long ago the following authentic case of Possession was communicated to the Editor of " Rome " by the Rt. Rev. Mgr. Delalle, Titular Bishop of Natal, Africa. The Bishop wrote:

" Two months ago I promised the Editor of ' Rome ' an account of certain facts which happened in my Vicariate last year (May, 1907), concerning two native girls whom I believe to have been possessed by the Devil.

" I shall simply relate the facts, without a word of comment, and shall content myself with vouching for their absolute truth. If anyone thinks differently from me on the subject he is quite free to do so; I mean, provided he admits the facts, he may draw his own conclusions.

" There is in the Vicariate of Natal a Mission, now in charge of the Trappist Fathers, where a great deal of good is done, although it was a long time before any results could be seen. This Mission is dedicated to St. Michael, and about twenty miles from the nearest village, the magistracy of Umzinto.

" For several months, I was constantly receiving letters from the priest in charge of St. Michael's, in which he declared that two girls of the Mission Native School were possessed by the devil, and asked for permission to practice the solemn Exorcisms. After some time, I allowed him to do so, and things were quieter for a little while, but soon the distressing phenomena reappeared worse than before. I was very much annoyed, and hardly believed it was a case of possession, but rather put it down to hysterics. Unable to go at the time, I gave permission to the Abbot of Marianhill either to go himself or delegate a priest who would enquire into the facts, and, if necessary, exorcise the girls. But a few days after, I found I could go myself, and wrote to St. Michael's, telling the priest to expect me on the Tuesday following; I should be accompanied by Father Garrigan, of Umzinto.

At the last moment, I changed my mind as to my travelling companion, and took Father Delagues, O.M.I., then in charge of the Native Mission in Durban.

"We set out on the Monday, and arrived at St. Michael's on Tuesday at noon.

"I really did not believe it was a case of possession, and Father Delagues laughed at the very idea of it.

"You may imagine, therefore, my annoyance, when on arriving at the Mission, I found the natives in eager expectation; the priest had told them that the Bishop was coming to cast out the devils, and prayers had been said every day for that intention. I had, therefore, unless I wanted to lose all prestige and authority in the natives' mind, to settle the case one way or the other. So I turned to Our Lord, and told Him the whole thing was now His affair, and He had to help me.

"We then went to see the two girls, Germana and Monica, who were kept in separate rooms, and away from the other children. As soon as Germana saw me, she began to tremble and shake all over, shrinking from me. I told her to kneel down, which she did gnashing her teeth. Father Delagues threatened to punish her, if she did not behave

85

properly; he had no sooner said this, than she jumped up, in a perfect fury:

" ' Because you are from Durban,' she said, ' you think you can do everything, even strike a spirit !'

" (Please note that she did not know the priest, neither did she know from whence he came.) She then began to tear her dress, and we went away to see Monica. The latter seemed to suffer terribly, but said nothing.

" I was very uncertain yet, and called the priests (three Trappists) and also the Sisters, and asked them some particulars about the ways of the two girls. Here are some of the things they told me:

" They carry enormous weights, which two men could hardly lift (the girls are about sixteen years old).

" They understand Latin whilst in their fits, and even speak it sometimes.

" They reveal the secret sins of the school children, etc.

" Sometimes they are lifted off the ground in spite of the Sisters holding them.

" A few days before, whilst the Sisters were holding Germana, she shouted:

" ' I am on fire !'

" The Sisters withdrew, and saw the girl's dress ablaze. Another time, her bed began to burn also, although there was no fire near by.

" And so on.

" It was getting very serious, and the poor Sisters, weary of this terrible life, begged of me to help them. After all this, I thought it was my duty to begin the solemn Exorcisms. I ordered the four priests and three Sisters to be ready to begin at 2 p.m., in the Sisters' Choir, and excluded everyone else from the Church. Just before the time, I had the Holy Water Font emptied and filled with plain water, whilst I took a small bottle of Holy Water in my pocket. Then I put on the rochet and mozetta, and waited for Germana.

" The Sisters brought her into the Chapel, and I sprinkled her at once with water from the font. At first, she looked up with a slight shudder, but as I continued, she laughed mockingly, and cried:

" ' You may go on, this is not Holy Water !'

" I then took the bottle out of my pocket and sprinkled her anew, but this time she shrieked and cried, and asked me to stop.

" Now, I must remark that all the time which the ordeal lasted, I spoke Latin only, the girl obeying all my orders, and answering me, usually in Zulu, but sometimes in Latin.

" After some prayers, I asked her : ' Dic mihi quomodo voceris ?', to which she replied : ' Dic mihi nomen tuum !' I insisted, and she said :

" ' I know your name, it is Henry, but where did you see that spirits have names ?'

" ' They have, and I command you to tell me yours.'

" ' Never, never !'

" But on my placing on her head a relic of the True Cross, which she could not see :

" ' Take that away,' she cried, ' it crushes me !' "

" ' What is it ?'

" ' A relic !'

" ' Then now tell me your name.'

" ' I can't, but I'll spell it: D-i-o-a-r.'

" ' Now, who is your master ?'

" ' I have none !'

" ' But you have one, and must tell me his name.'

" ' I cannot, but I shall write it,' and she wrote with her finger: ' Lucifer.'

" ' Now,' I went on, ' tell me why you were cast out from Heaven.'

" ' Because God showed us His Son made man, and commanded us to adore Him; but we would not, because He had taken unto Himself an inferior nature.'

" Whilst I was going on with the prayers of the ritual, she (should I not say he? however, you understand) interrupted me constantly, objecting to all the invocations. When I read extracts from the Gospels, she suddenly exclaimed:

" ' I know Matthew, I don't know Mark !'

" ' This is an untruth, and to make up for it kneel down at once.'

" Which she did. Whilst we recited the Magnificat, she interrupted again:

89

"'Stop it, I know it better than you, I knew it long before you were born!'

"As one of the Fathers commanded her to be quiet, she turned on him:

"'You fool! who gave you authority over me? Did the Bishop or the Abbot delegate you?'

"At times she remained quiet and disdainful; but sometimes she raged and gnashed her teeth: 'I'll make you sweat before I get out,' she said once; then all of a sudden she begged to be allowed to go in to another girl, Anastasia:

"'Stop your prayers,' she said, 'they hurt me; if you stop, I shall go out to-morrow morning!'

"Time went on, and, as I was tired, I commissioned one of the priests to read the prayers for me. He did so, but with a droning voice; as he stopped at the end of a paragraph, she turned fiercely upon him:

"'Exi, immunde, spiritus!' she said.

"From time to time, she went into awful fits of roaring; on such occasions I had only to place two fingers lightly on the throat, and she could not utter a sound. To make a counter-experiment, I asked one of the Sisters to do the same as I did, but it had no effect:

" ' Tell me,' I said, ' why you are so much afraid of the priest's fingers?'

" ' Because,' she answered, ' they are consecrated,' and she made the motion of the Bishop anointing the priest's hands at his ordination.

" We went on thus from 2 p.m. until 9 o'clock in the evening, when I decided to stop till the following morning.

" Afterwards Germana was somewhat quieter, and she came, begging of me not to give her up: ' I am sure,' she said, ' that if you said your Mass for me to-morrow, it would be easier.'

" ' Yes,' I answered, ' I shall, but on the condition that you will go to Confession and Communion to-morrow morning.'

" The night was awful, and the poor Sisters had to remain with her all through. She went to Confession and Holy Communion in the morning, and remained quiet until at 8.30 we began the Exorcisms again.

91

" From the very first words she became unmanageable, and we had to tie her feet and her hands, since eight of us could not control her.

" ' You have sent away Anastasia,' she cried. ' I can see her with another girl on their way to another mission, but I'll find her again.'

" It was true, early in the morning I had sent her away, but Germana could not possibly know of it. After a while, someone called a priest away; he came back half-an-hour later.

" ' Where has he been ?' I asked.

" ' He went to baptize a man who got sick suddenly.'

" That also was true, though nobody in the chapel knew it.

" Then she asked for a drink, and some one of us fetched her a cup of water. After drinking some of it she stopped:

" ' Wretched men,' she said, ' you gave me holy water !'

" Still I made her drink the whole of it, and she became quite defiant.

" ' All right, give me more still, it will not make me suffer more than I do.'

" It would be too long, were I to repeat everything she said. Suffice it to say, that every moment it became more and more awful, until at last she tried to bite a priest. He, somewhat excited, gave her a little tap on the mouth, at which she became worse, and called him the most stupid of men, who wanted to strike a spirit. As I commanded her to keep quiet, she cried: ' Now, no more obedience !'

" It was the end, evidently, but the struggle was terrible. At last, she fell to the floor, and moaned with awful pains. Her face swelled up suddenly, so that she could not even open her eyes, and the tears came down her cheeks. But the sign of the cross brought the face instantly back to its natural size.

" Then a kind of convulsion, and she remained motionless, as if dead. Locus vero foetore redolebat. After about ten minutes, she opened her eyes, and knelt down to thank God. She was released. ' Dioar ' had gone.

" This is the summary of what happened to Germana. If anyone can explain the signs,

93

the symptoms, the words, and the cure, otherwise than by possession, he will be more clever than I am.

" I shall perhaps relate some other time the case of Monica, and, in the meantime, I give the Editor of ' Rome ' leave to do with this what he likes.

" I have in my possession a letter sent me by Germana afterwards in which she begs that I may pray for her death. She has seen too much, and is afraid of life."

XXX.

It is surely instructive to note, in this connection, that the form of words which the Catholic Church uses in blessing holy water is as follows:

" I exorcise thee, O creature of water, in the name of God the Father Almighty, in the name of Jesus Christ His Son our Lord, and in the power of the Holy Ghost, that you become exorcised water to put to flight every power of the enemy, and that you may eradicate and expel (explantare) the enemy himself with his apostatized angels, by the

94

power of the same Lord . . . . Jesus Christ."

XXXI.

And as unmistakeable signs of obsession or possession by evil spirits the Church has always regarded:

1. The power of knowing the unexpressed thoughts of others.

2. The understanding of unknown languages.

3. The power of speaking unknown or foreign languages.

4. The knowledge of future events.

5. The knowledge of things passing in distant places.

6. The exhibition of abnormal physical strength.

7. The suspension of the body in the air during a considerable time (in imitation of a similar phenomenon observed in the lives of the Saints.)

8. Hatred of saintly persons, of the ordained, of Sacraments and Sacramentalia, even of

95

near relatives; persistent impulse to suicide. A safe sign (according to Poullain) is persistent opposition to the exorcist, so different from submission to the hypnotist.

XXXII.

An Australian priest whom I met in Rome some years ago and who confessed to a naturally sceptical attitude respecting the ordinary accounts of the preternatural, had become a believer by reason of the following occurrence. (It will be borne in mind that similar occurrences, observed by himself, were instrumental in breaking down the scientific scepticism of the late Professor Lombroso.)

Father P. was told by some friends that the house in which they were living was haunted. They heard footsteps and other inexplicable noises after the members of the household had retired to rest. Father P. at first discredited the story, and thought that the noises could probably be explained by some natural cause. Upon renewed assurances, however, that this could not be the case, he proceeded to bless the place with the sanction of the Bishop. But the noises continued, matters becoming worse rather than better. About that time a deaf and dumb child, who had also been born blind, was being sent through the town to be received into a neighbouring Home. Having to find a bed for her, and feeling that her infirmity would make it impossible for her to be subjected to these annoyances, she was placed in this room. At night she came rushing out of the room with every sign of extreme fear and alarm. Father P. then made a novena with the inhabitants of the house, after which the disturbance ceased entirely.

When our sceptical neurologists can adequately explain authenticated occurrences of this kind, whose number is legion, it will be time for us to take their scepticism seriously. In view of the testimony available to-day simple denial of such occurrences is not likely to serve them much longer.

When my book, " The Dangers of Spiritualism," was first published, I received many letters of enquiry and suggestion from correspondents who were keenly interested in the case of M., whose sad history I have recorded in that book.

It was a case of playing with " planchette " as an apparently innocent after-dinner amusement, which, however, ended in obsession of a peculiarly painful and repulsive type. I had the case under observation for a considerable time, and did my utmost to relieve the poor victim of the dreadful invasion. He was, however, too terrified to submit himself to the process of exorcism. I lost sight of him after that. His last words to me were " I shall either become insane or commit suicide." I heard incidentally last year that the latter had actually occurred.

XXIII.

The late Judge Edmonds, of New York, made the following public statement respecting his daughter* :—

" She knows no language but her own and a little smattering of boarding-school French; yet she has spoken in nine or ten different tongues, often for an hour at a time, with the

*See his published account.

ease and fluency of a native. It is not
unfrequent that foreigners converse with their
spirit-friends through her in their own
language."

Many years ago, in my pre-Catholic days, I
was present at a gathering where a spirit,
communicating through an entranced medium,
spoke to a member of my family in Hindustani.
The lady had lived in India, and had on one
occasion punished and dismissed a native
servant, and the spirit, claiming to be this
servant, referred to this occurrence in an
intelligent manner. It is scarcely necessary to
add that the medium was a stranger to this lady,
and that no person present could by any stretch
of the imagination have had knowledge of the
circumstances of the case.

I do not think that, in view of the systematic
study of these phenomena in recent times and
of the rapidly increasing evidence, it is necessary
to give much consideration to the statements of
some psychologists who are still labouring
under conventional preconceptions and anti-
quated views. Their position is becoming daily

more untenable. It would seem to require no very high degree of intelligence to see at a glance that phenomena of the kind described cannot be fitted into any theory of duplex or dissociated personality. The men who still advance these theories have never seen true spiritistic phenomena. We have to-day the testimony of trained medical and scientific experts who are not only well acquainted with the phenomena of mental dissociation and with the various forms of sub-conscious mind-activity but who have also patiently and carefully studied spiritistic manifestations. It was often quite contrary to their expectations and to their personal leanings that they were driven to their affirmative conclusions. And once arrived at such conclusions, the further inference becomes almost inevitable.

Justly writes the American experimenter, Prof. Hyslop:

"It ought to be apparent that the assumption of a spiritistic hypothesis increases the possibilities of obsession."

XXXIV.

But, in order to leave no doubt on these points in the mind of any reader, I submit the following statements. *Scientific and other Testimonies.*

Dr. Joseph Venzano, an eminent and well-known medical man, whose name has been associated for many years with psychical research in Italy and who is beyond doubt one of the most cautious and painstaking investigators, writes* :

" In this connection we have not thought it necessary to consider the theory of psychic dissociation of personality which Dr. Pierre Janet constructed upon the masterly observations made by him upon various subjects in a state of hypnotic somnambulism.

" Such a theory is in no way applicable to our case, for the following reasons. Dissociations of personality, as Dr. Janet has shown, can give rise to real individualisations, but these resulting personalities are only secondary ones, with limited intellectual faculties. Moreover, *they are only portions of*

Annals of Psychical Science. Sept., 1907, pp. 185, 186.

a disrupted consciousness, so that the greater the dissociation, the less is the psychic activity of the normal consciousness. The proof of what we have just said is the fact that, when the dissociated faculties are capable of composing a complete subconscious personality, endowed with a certain amount of independence, the normal personality is so impoverished that it cannot subsist as an entity, and the subject falls into a deep sleep, thus permitting the sub-hypnotic personality to emerge.

" Nothing of this sort, as we see, is to be met with in the phenomena we have described. The personalities who manifest, not only appear as materialised forms, visible and tangible, but are gifted with intellectual faculties which are the reverse of small, and which reflect the feelings and affections of the individuals which they claim to represent, calling up with wonderful correctness circumstances and details of the facts *unknown to the medium,* known to few of us, and sometimes even long forgotten.

" Moreover, these personalities, though they often reveal themselves whilst E—— is in trance, *appear also when she is perfectly awake*, in full mental self-possession, in such a way as to take a keen interest in the phenomena which are being developed through her mediumship. Consequently the hypothesis of possible mental dissociation cannot be advanced with regard to the phenomena which we have described, and we have thought it unnecessary to refer to it when discussing them."

XXXV.

Mr. Ernest Bozzano, another scientist student of the phenomena, comes to the same conclusion* :

" It must not be supposed that these are instances of contrary personalities, such as appertain to many psycho-pathological subjects who, during the hallucinatory trance, are often in constant struggle with individualities which are merely the product of their diseased brains.   The personalities

*Annals, p. 187.

described by us, with which the will of the medium is in conflict, are not the product of hallucinated brains; they are actual personifications, which can be rendered objective, either to sight, or contact or hearing; they are real creations having the aspect of a human form."

XXXVI.

Dr. G. B. Ermacora, of Padua, another Italian savant, who has made a thorough-going study of psychic phenomena, writes†:

" The subconscious ' personalities ' are wholly devoid of transcendental characteristics. They are scattered fragments of the person's mind, and merely reflect its normal powers, although these are often overstrained in some particular direction."

" The personalities (of the spiritistic séance). convey information which could never have reached the medium or any person present at the communication; they sometimes predict future events with extraordinary accuracy,

†In an article, entitled *Transcendental Activity and Spiritism,* a German translation of which is published in Leipzig.

talk or write in languages unknown to any person present and, according to the testimony of persons worthy of every confidence, produce the most marvellous physical phenomena. Amongst these are direct writing, the instantaneous apport of articles from a distance of several kilometres, and their passage through solid walls held by physical science to be impenetrable. Besides this they allow themselves to be seen in human form, not by some kind of subjective perception (hallucination), but objectively as really living human bodies, which can be weighed and photographed and whose members leave impressions on flour, or blackened paper, and yield the most perfect impression on paraffin.''

XXXVII.

And although it is scarcely necessary, at this hour of the day, seriously to consider the theory of fraud in connection with the spirit-phenomena here referred to, the following note may be added for the benefit of those who may be imperfectly acquainted with the available evidence. Dr. Venzano writes respecting the reality of the spiritistic manifestations observed in Italy*:—

"The hypothesis (that of fraud) which we have suggested is, therefore, not logically possible. And if we thus exclude it, it is easy to see that that of an illusion of the senses cannot be entertained either. The *duration* of the apparitions, the perfect agreement of all the experimenters in observing them, *the shadows they cast on the walls of the gas-lighted room*, all serve to disprove every possibility of hallucination. One of the most striking peculiarities of the materialisations observed, is that they appeared and *remained visible for some time in such brilliant gaslight* that it was possible, as Prof. Morselli observed, to read even the small print of a newspaper."

XXXVIII.

It is perhaps not generally known that the late Professor C. Lombroso made a personal and extensive investigation of haunted houses.

Annals. Sept., 1907.

He approached the subject, as may be imagined, with the sceptical mental attitude of the modern savant, but, having opportunities of witnessing manifestations which took place in his presence, *in the daylight and without the presence of a sensitive,* he was driven to an affirmative conclusion. And, unlike some of his confrères, he had the courage of his convictions. In an article on " Haunted Houses," contributed to " The Annals of Psychical Science," he wrote :

" It is very curious to note how we have been able, in recent years, to verify such a number of facts, with documentary evidence, while for nearly two centuries none were placed on record, except among the lowest classes of the people, who were, we might say, scarcely in communication with the cultivated classes. At all events, the latter, not believing in them when they occurred before their very eyes, took no pains to examine into them and to make their existence known, so that the memory of them was lost. Now, when they occur, they are noticed and studied; though even now they are easily forgotten, and meet only with incredulity and derision. Thus, in

107

the Fumero case, if I had not persisted and returned to the place, it would have been believed that on the first appearance of the police or myself on the scene, the phenomena had ceased, and they would easily have been attributed to a trick, thus turning away from them all serious attention."

XXXIX.

Con-clusions and Infer-ences.

It will thus be seen that the evidence for the existence and operation of unseen spirit-agencies is now as complete as the most sceptical mind can desire it to be. Indeed it is as perfect as it is ever likely to be. This fact can only be doubted by those who have not made themselves acquainted with the evidence or who gather their information from the newspapers or from popular scientific or non-scientific literature. I have had opportunities of discussing the subject with experts in all parts of the world, and I have not found that doubt on this point existed in any single instance. The burning question of the hour really is: What is the nature and aim of the intelligences who are disclosing themselves by means of these phenomena?

XL.

I have, I think, shown in my previous writings that the popular spiritistic theory—that these spirits are the souls of the dead—cannot be held where *all* the facts of the case are fairly and fully considered. Indeed an increasing number of scientific investigators have come to this conclusion, and are, in their statements, approaching the Catholic theory. Nearly all of them are cautious in their utterances on this point, and are warning against the dangers attending spiritistic practices. It may be confidently asserted that still further research will tend to show the entire reasonableness of this theory, even from the scientific point of view, and that the time is not far distant when the Catholic Church will be admitted to possess the only true key to the solution of the spiritistic problem. But, lest an impression should be created that Catholic writers manipulate the evidence in order to prove the reasonableness of their Church's teaching, I will add the following notes from the pens of non-Catholic writers:

XLI.

In a letter on " The Dangers of Spiritism and Black Magic," recently published by " The Outlook," a correspondent who is evidently well acquainted with the subject and whose aim is not the defence of the Historic Christian Faith, writes as follows:

" Spirit-obsession is one of the commonest troubles the race is suffering from. . . . Of course the great difficulty is that the whole thing is generally regarded as a phantasma or hallucination: unfortunately it is far from being so. The miserable victims generally become aware of a dual force in their lives. Religion, if they have any, is generally wiped clean out. A sense of despair and loss of self-confidence takes its place. The field offers an interesting scope for investigation. On the face of it the whole thing is strenuously denied; but those who are behind the scenes and have examined all the evidence bit by bit have no other option but to accept the truth of the present phenomena."

XLII.

Some years ago the Protestant missionary, Dr. Nevius, published an interesting work, entitled "Demon Possession and Allied Themes," being an inductive study of Phenomena of our own times. The "Psychological Review," in calling attention to this important work, had the following:

"This interesting contribution to mental pathology would probably, fifteen years ago, have gained for its author a reputation for nothing but mendacity or childish credulity in scientific circles; but now, thanks to the 'apperceiving mass' which recent investigations into trance-conditions have prepared, probably few readers of this journal will be seriously tempted to doubt its being a trustworthy report of facts. Dr. Nevius, for forty years a missionary in China, who died in 1893, is described by Drs. Ellinwood and Rankin as a man of rare learning, versatility and integrity. From the beginning of his sojourn in China his attention was attracted to the popular belief in demons and spirits. He found before long that the native converts very uncommonly believed in demoniacal possession and in the power of Christian rites and invocations to exorcise the spirit. In 1878 he met with his first case, that of a non-Christian native named Kwo, who, having bought a picture of the goddess Wang, had been visited by a demon-counterfeit of the goddess in a dream, who told him she had taken up her abode in his house. Various neurotic conditions and disorderly impulses had followed, ending in an attack of frenzy during which, the man being unconscious, the demon spoke through his lips, demanding incense, worship, etc. As usual, the demands were met by the family, and the pacified demon thereafter made periodical visitations, throwing the man into unconsciousness and speaking through his organism, healing the diseases of visitors, and giving practical advice. On Dr. Nevius assuring Kwo that conversion to Christianity would rid him of the encumbrance, he became baptized, the trance-state only recurring once afterwards, and the demon bidding a formal farewell on that occasion. Fourteen years have passed without relapse. Kwo has had persecutions and trials, but no return of his malady, and neither he nor his neighbours think of doubting that he was rescued from the dominion of an evil spirit through faith and trust in Christ.

" This case can serve as a type. Dr. Nevius has personally observed several others, and collected a large amount of information on the subject from other missionaries and from native Christians. The possessed persons are unconscious during the attacks, which have often, though not always, a convulsive character. The possessing spirit usually names itself, often as a deity, sometimes as a departed human being, and demeans itself accordingly. Sometimes it makes a formal treaty to behave well, on condition of certain favours being granted it. Sometimes it is driven out by threats or needle-pricks, etc. Christian rites seem to have extraordinary exorcising efficacy. . . . . The phenomena are among the most constant in history, and it is most extraordinary that ' Science ' should ever have become blind to them," etc.

113

XLIII.

In their attempts to contravene and disprove the demonic interpretation of modern spiritistic phenomena, it is asserted that spirits of this nature would display uniform power and intelligence, and would not commit blunders such as are known to be committed in the course of communication: but they forget that S. Thomas Aquinas already taught that a certain order exists amongst the evil spirits, and that some are naturally more perfect and powerful than others. And the more intelligent and powerful ones would thus lead and rule the inferior ones.*

XLIV.

There is certainly an intelligible point of view from which we come to understand why the malignant power of these spirits is so often absent from experiments carried on by scientific men and by the expounders of popular spiritism. Indeed this view is based upon admissions which have been obtained from time to time from the

*See *The Unseen World,* by the Very Rev. A. M. Lépicier, O.S.M.

spirits themselves. Would they not frustrate their own designs if they allowed the whole truth to become known? Would not scientific men either shut the door once for all upon these investigations, or themselves be strongly influenced in the true supernatural direction? " Compelled to acknowledge the existence of satan, they might go further and acknowledge that of Christ and become Christians."* In any case it is certain that by the present attitude of continued research and of fresh and ingenious attempts to establish spirit-identity, the door of communication between the two states is kept wide open, and thousands of unwary persons, who only know the interesting side of these experiments, are drawn into spiritistic practices.

XLV.

What the aim of these spirits is in seeking to impress the world with the idea that they are the spirits of the dead who have survived the shock of physical dissolution and who have important communications to make respecting the future

*Brownson : *The Spirit Rapper*, p. 355.

life, should become clear upon very little reflection. It is best expressed in the words of a former spiritist:

" If they would tell us who they were at first, no Christian would be led to depart from the faith by their false teaching; but if they can by any means lead us to believe that the spirit of a dear mother, father, companion, brother or sister, who died happy in the Lord, has come to visit us, of course we should not fear that they would guide us wrong, seeing that they manifested so much interest in our welfare while living here. This constitutes the deception. They pretend to be the spirits of dear friends, and to convince us of this they give us good advice, and seduce us by their fair words; then, step by step, they lead us away from the road to life eternal into the broad way to destruction."

XLVI.

But it must not be supposed that the occult and spiritistic practices of modern times furnish us with the only reliable evidence of the presence

and operation of malignant spirits. The entire
history of mankind and of the Church, the
hypnotic experiments of modern times, the study
of phenomena occurring in haunted houses and
of those presenting themselves in connection
with some apparently insane persons, reveal the
constant interference in the life of man of
agencies who, in one way or another, discover
the means of access to him. The experiments
referred to most certainly constitute "open
doors" by which that access is facilitated and
rendered a close and personal one. All forms of
unhealthy and abnormal mind-passivity may be
regarded as such "open doors." Certain forms
of mental and physical disease too and all forms
of vice and sin are by many ancient and modern
writers regarded in this light. All such states
and conditions decrease the natural powers of
resistance and enable these hostile forces*, by a
kind of telepathic influence to invade the mental
and moral life, without the operation being even
suspected by the victim. It is unfortunately
only in quite recent times that this aspect of the
matter has received serious scientific attention;

*Ephes. vi., 12.

117

but one cannot doubt that the time is not far distant when its closer and fuller study will enable us to explain much that is still so perplexing and mysterious in the moral life of man.

XLVII.

Demonic Activity in "Heroic Forms of Sanctity." There is one form of spirit-invasion, of the reality of which there cannot be any possible doubt and of which mention should be made in this connection. We may trace this kind of invasion throughout the history of the Catholic Church, and it would seem to be an element which frequently accompanies the higher developments of the spiritual life and the cultivation of what the Church terms " heroic forms of sanctity." In any case it is important not to confound this kind of spirit invasion or obsession with that which is the result of human experiment and initiative.

XLVIII.

All spiritual and mystic writers agree that some forms of obsession may be regarded as indications of God's favour. They constitute a

118

kind of conflict in which God gives to the demons exceptional power and permission to tempt man, while He lays upon man the duty to suffer and to endure. The result of a conflict of this kind is marked spiritual progress. With the certainty which is thus furnished to the soul of the presence and activity of these hostile forces, the soul is correspondingly strengthened and energized. Dormant and hitherto unused spiritual powers and possibilities are awakened. While the demons thus conquer in the lower sphere of the soul's life, they are conquered in the higher.*

St. Paul speaks of a person delivered " to satan for the destruction of the flesh that the spirit may be saved in the day of our Lord Jesus Christ."†

Thus all exceptional or heroic spiritual efforts at sanctity provoke exceptional demonic activity. The cold and indifferent only are left alone. The less frequent occurrence, therefore, of this class of phenomena in our age is not due, as some Protestant theologians imagine, to the circum-

*II. Cor., xii., 7-10.
†I. Cor. v., 5.

119

stance that demonic action has ceased, but because God does not regard a lukewarm or apostate world worthy even of this.

XLIX.

Scaramelli, probably the greatest authority on Mystical Theology, tells us that Maria Crucifixa, the method of whose purification was of so severe and painful a character, was sometimes inspired with heretical ideas which were so convincing that one would imagine she had learned them in the schools of the heretics. *And yet she had never read of these things or even heard them spoken of.**

"Sometimes," he says, "the enemy takes advantage of a state of sadness in which a person may find himself, in order to inspire the soul with heretical principles. In a state of dryness, for instance, he suggests the idea that God is cruel and unjust, since He deals so hardly with souls that are eager to serve Him faithfully, first attracting them with the sweetness of consolation, in order to treat them with cruelty afterwards."

Mystical Theology.

Again he writes† :

" He (the devil) creates in the soul the most violent doubts against Faith, suggests to the mind the most plausible arguments against the truths of the Catholic Religion—against the existence of God, the mystery of the most holy Trinity, the purity of the Blessed Virgin, the immortality of the soul and eternal life. And he does this by powerfully inviting them to lead a gay life and to delight in the abominable thought that after death there is neither punishment nor reward. He makes a special effort to undermine belief in the holy Sacraments, especially in the most holy Sacrament of the altar, with respect to which he infuses into the mind such false, blasphemous and absolutely contemptible thoughts that the soul loses all faith in and love for It and finally withdraws from It altogether."

L.

Sometimes demonic invasions of this kind take an external form as well as an internal one, and

†*Mystic Theology.*

are of so manifest and violent a character that no possible doubt can remain as to the extraneous and malignant character of the agency which is at work. The lives of the Saints record many visitations of this kind. But here too the invasion generally precedes the bestowal of some signal and exceptional blessing and, in the hands of God, becomes an effective means of confirming the faith and fortifying the soul of His servant. One of the best-known and best-attested instances of this kind of demonic activity is that recorded in the life of the saintly Curé d'Ars who declared repeatedly that a " pounding " given to him by these demonic beings " was always followed by something good."

The Abbe Monnin, his biographer, writes*:

" The vexations which he endured from the demon formed the subject of frequent conversation among the Clergy present, who amused themselves much at his expense. ' Come, come, dear curé; do like other people, feed better; it is the only way to put an end to all this diablerie."

*Life of the Curé d'Ars

"One evening his critics took a higher tone; the discussion waxed warm on their side, and the raillery grew more bitter and less restrained. It was agreed that all this infernal mysticism was nothing in the world but reverie, delusion and hallucination; and the poor curé was openly treated as a visionary and a maniac. 'Your presbytery,' said they, 'is nothing better than an old barn, without either order or arrangement. The rats are quite at home there; they play their pranks night and day, and you take them for devils.' The good Curé said not a word in reply to these sage admonitions, but retired to his room, rejoicing in the humiliation."

"A few moments afterwards those who had been so witty at his expense wished each other good-night, and retired also to their respective apartments, with the happy indifference of philosophers, who, if they believed in the devil at all, had very little faith in his intermeddling with the affairs of the Curé of Ars. But, behold! at midnight they are awakened by a most terrible commotion. The presbytery is turned upside down, the doors slam, the windows rattle, the walls shake, and fearful cracks seem to betoken that they are about to fall prostrate. Every one was out of bed in a moment. They remembered that the Curé of Ars had said: " You will not be astonished if you should happen to hear a noise to-night."

" Get up," they cry; "the presbytery is falling !"

" Oh, I know very well what it is," replied he, smiling. " Go to your beds; there is nothing to fear."

" They were re-assured, and the noise ceased. An hour afterwards, when all was quiet, a gentle ring was heard at the door. The Abbé Vianney rose, and found a man at the door, who had walked many miles in order to make his confession to him. He went at once to the Church, and remained there hearing the confessions of a great number of penitents, until it was time for Mass." One of the missionaries, M. l'Abbé Chevalon, of pious memory, an old soldier of the Empire, was so struck by this strange adventure, that he said, when relating it, " I made a promise to our Lord never again to jest about these

stories of apparitions and nightly disturb-
ances; and as to the Curé of Ars, I take him
to be a saint."

" The coincidence of the occurrence of these
noises with the arrival of the penitent for confession, is one instance out of many in which
a more than usual manifestation of diabolical
fury proved the presage of some more than
common manifestation of the Divine mercy to
sinners. M. Vianney would often rise, after a
harrassed and sleepless night, to find strangers
waiting at the door, who had travelled all
night to make their confession."

LI.

With really reflecting persons the difficulty
which presents itself in connection with an
occurrence of this kind is probably not the
existence of the devil. There is surely nothing
against reason, on the contrary it is in entire
keeping with reason, to conclude that if evil
spirits exist in this mysterious universe, they
should have a chief or superior who, by reason
of his superior intellectual powers, has gained an

ascendancy over them and become their leader. The difficulty which most people experience would probably formulate itself thus : Why does not God exercise His almighty power and destroy this rebellious angel? But this surely would be a thing inconceivable. God clearly had a plan in the creation of the universe, seen and unseen. From this plan a departure cannot be conceived because of the action of one of the beings created; for God would then be submitting to the will of His creatures—indeed His action would be modified by that of the creature —God ceasing to be God.

The rationalising Protestant theology of our days is seeking to get over the difficulty by denying the existence of the devil as a personal living and acting entity. But it must surely be seen that, however strongly this method may appeal to and fit in with the " Zeitgeist," it leaves a hundred problems unsolved and indeed but increases our intellectual perplexity. It wholly fails, moreover, to offer an adequate explanation of well-attested occurrences of this kind. Acceptance of the emphatic teaching of our Lord, upon which the teaching of the

Catholic Church is based and which her experience throughout the centuries most amply confirms, alone fully and satisfactorily explains them.

LII.

And experience tends to show that whenever the mind's hold upon the belief in an active malignant power in the universe is relaxed, a corresponding relaxation of the mind's hold upon the *supernatural* truths of Christianity is apt to result. This again leads to a dangerous laxness in the spiritual life —a falling back upon purely natural means for the defence and safeguarding of the soul. But natural means and remedies cannot help us much, if there are assaults upon the soul, interior conflicts and struggles, which have a preternatural cause. We must then put on " the whole armour of God " if we are to be effectively protected against them.*

*Ephes. vi., 10, &c.

127

LIII.

In view of the false ideas which are current in our time it cannot be emphasized too frequently that the New Testament clearly distinguishes between disease and the operation of evil spirits. We read in St. Mark's Gospel† :

"He healed many troubles with divers diseases, and He cast out many devils, and He suffered them not to speak because they knew Him."

And the Church in all ages has not only equally distinguished between these two conditions; she has also distinguished between obsession and possession, and has investigated with care before pronouncing judgment. Sufferers were confined in houses, instituted for the purpose, where they could be kept under constant observation, and where both moral and physical remedies and modes of treatment could be resorted to. When obsession or possession had been diagnosed and deliverance had been effected by exorcism, aided by the prayers of the faithful, the afflicted person remained some time under the observation of the exorcist.

†Ch. i., 34.

Very wisely writes Scaramelli:

" As those persons who are besieged and persecuted by demons, are also, like other people, subject to those natural ailments which are not due to the devil and which can be remedied by natural means, the difficult problem presents itself how the former are to be distinguished from the latter.

" When doubts of this kind present themselves I would advise the spiritual director to judge the matter for himself, and not to resort to the decision of medical men; for these as a rule have no experience of these purifications and extraordinary ways along which God is leading select souls. They ascribe everything to nature, and imagine that they can relieve the evil with their remedies. Thus grave mistakes are apt to be made which are often disastrous to the bodily well-being of the poor penitent."*

LIV.

Scaramelli further points out that although in the Latin and Italian languages the one word *obsessus* is used in describing both conditions,

Mystic Theology.

the scholastics and mystics have always distinguished between the two. "Demonic possession," he says, "consists in a despotic power which the devil exercises over the senses and bodily constitution (humours) of a person, despite that person's resistance and opposition." The demon is *in* the person in the same way in which he was in the idols of the heathen.

*Pos*session is not inflicted upon those whom God desires to lead on to perfection; but upon the wicked whom He wants to punish.

LV.

St. Thomas too defines POSSESSION as a *union* of the demon with the body of the possessed *into which he enters*. He (the demon) uses his organs and exercises control over their functions as though they were his own.*

In OBSESSION, on the other hand, the devil's action is compared to that of a general who, with his army, surrounds a city, disquiets and troubles it, and occasionally penetrates into it, but does not actually occupy it.

*See St. Matth. viii., 28 · ix., 32, 33 ; xii. 22 ; xvii., 14.

LVI.

Evil spirits, it may here be pointed out, are limited and finite in their knowledge, operation and powers and can only hurt and tempt man as far as God permits. Without Christ's permission they could not even hurt swine. Reflection shows that in these operations there is nothing incongruous or unjust. We are beings who with one side of their nature stand in the material world, and are there exposed to the good and evil influences of their fellowmen. With the other side of their nature they stand in the spiritual world where they are exposed to the influence of good and evil spirits.

These may thus become God's instruments by which He executes justice or punishes sin. No man, therefore, is secure from the temptations of the devil; but it must be evident that the unbaptized, and persons in a state of grievous sin, are particularly exposed to the influence of evil spirits. Nowhere is this more forcibly explained than in the prayers and ceremonies which the Church uses in Holy Baptism.

Exorcism and Exorcists. The following sentences, taken from the Roman Ritual, will clearly indicate the Church's mind and teaching in this respect:

No. 3. " Go out from him (or her), unclean spirit, and give place to the Holy Spirit Comforter (Paraclete.")

(This is said by the priest when he blows upon the face of the recipient of Holy Baptism.)

No. 7. " I exorcise thee, unclean spirit, in the name of the Father+and of the Son+and of the Holy Ghost+that thou go out and withdraw from this servant of God N.—. For He Whose feet walked the sea and Whose right hand was stretched out to Peter as he sank, Himself commands thee, thou damned and accursed one. Acknowledge then, thou devil accursed, thy sentence (condemnation) and give honour to the living and true God, to Jesus Christ His Son, and to the Holy Spirit, and withdraw from this servant of God N—, for him hath our God and Lord Jesus Christ deigned to call unto His holy grace and benediction and to the font of Baptism."

LVII.

In the Roman Ritual the following warning is given to the exorcist:

" Before all let him (the exorcist) not easily believe that anyone is obsessed by a demon; but let him know those signs by which an obsessed person is distinguished from such as suffer from melancholy (atra bilis) or some disease."

The chief signs are then given (see page 95). The Roman Pontifical directs:

" You . . . receive the power to lay hand on the possessed (energumeni) and by the grace of the Holy Ghost, and by the words of exorcism the impure spirits are driven from the possessed bodies."

LVIII.

The instructions to the exorcist himself, in preparation for his difficult task, were as follows:

1. There must be a right interior state and disposition which are attained by the purification of conscience, ascetical practices, and the generous use of the means of grace.

133

These latter are of a twofold character:

    (*a*) *ordinary* and *general* such as the use of the Sacraments and pious exercises of various kinds.

    (*b*) *extraordinary and specific*: exorcism, mortification, ascetical practices, etc., etc.

2. A General Confession.

3. Entire Confidence in God (on the part of both exorcist and sufferer).

4. The exorcism not to be attempted unless the conditions imposed have been fulfilled on both sides.

(The possibility of failure and of relapse was always kept in view).

An experienced spiritual writer further instructs the sufferer:

" There must be no argument with the enemy in the hope perhaps of convincing him of the truth, partly because of the superior and keen intelligence at work, partly because at such times the soul is wrapt in darkness and easily confused. All spiritual writers agree

134

that the one remedy is to despise the devil and to turn one's back on him and to direct heart and soul towards God, making lively acts of Faith in Him and in the truths of the Catholic Religion. ' Lord, I believe, help Thou mine unbelief.' ''

LIX.

In view of the preceding considerations it can scarcely be doubted that, besides the extra-ordinary and manifest instances of spirit-invasion referred to, an ordinary and less manifest spirit-activity is incessantly at work, striving to obstruct man's spiritual progress and seeking, by numerous and little-suspected devices, to enslave and entrap his soul. The holiest of men cannot hope to prevent the devil from suggesting evil to their minds through telepathic influence. This surely is what is meant by temptation, and the Sacred Scriptures especially teach that the whole of mankind is tempted in this way. Most careful students of the subject have come to the conclusion that assaults of this kind may occur through the

135

slightest cause, may even connect themselves with physical and mental disease, but more especially with sin, both venial and mortal.

Against this kind of assault it behoves us to be on our guard by employing the various means which the Church has devised for our aid and protection. We must not only bring our bodies into subjection by a well-ordered and well-directed discipline, but we must also employ those external and objective remedies which experience has proved to be effectual weapons in our warfare with the enemy. We must make a generous use of *the Sacramentalia* of the Church, such as Holy Water, Blessed Objects of various kinds, especially the Crucifix; we must not only seek the blessing of priests, but protect ourselves by the use of objects over which consecrating words have been uttered. Experience constantly teaches that there is far greater virtue and aid in these humble means of grace than is commonly supposed. We must bear in mind St. Paul's* words that it is by the weak and insignificant things that great things are effected in the spiritual order.

*I. Cor., i., 27.

136

LX.

It is quite astonishing to what admissions the spirits of the séance room, whose nature and statements are for the most part frivolous, and who love foolish jesting and repartee, will sometimes commit themselves. I was once, in my pre-Catholic days, asking questions of an apparently superior intelligence who seemed disposed to gratify my curiosity, and being at that time keenly interested in the teaching of the Catholic Church and yet struggling with inherited prejudices and misconceptions, I tried to ascertain how matters presented themselves from the spirit-side of life. My questions turned round the use of Sacramentals: In Catholic countries, I observed, especially in the humble villages of the Black Forest, there are few houses in which a crucifix is not placed in some prominent part of the living-room. It seems to be regarded as a talisman or charm by the people (I had observed this during a stay in the Black Forest while on a walking tour.) Is this merely a pious custom which is felt to be helpful to devotion; or does some special virtue or power emanate from or adhere to the sacred symbol?

137

The answer came with clearness and precision —to this effect. If the crucifix has been blessed by a priest an influence or aura adheres to it. Of this the spirits of the air, happening to pass through the house, or for some reason attracted to it, become conscious; they feel its influence, and as a consequence they pass on. They say to themselves: " It is no use staying here. These people are good Christians; they are protected by the Cross." I can only add that at this time I knew little or nothing of the Catholic teaching respecting Sacramentals.

LXI.

With regard to self-discipline and the governing of our bodies St. Teresa writes*:

" We may also imitate the saints by striving after solitude and silence, and many other virtues that will not kill these wretched bodies of ours, which insist on being treated so orderly, that they may disorder the soul; and satan, too, helps much to make them unmanageable. When he sees us a little

*Life of S. Teresa, written by herself; English Translation by David Lewis, p. 94.

138

anxious about them, he wants nothing more to convince us that our way of life must kill us and destroy our health, etc. . . .

" But when it pleased God to let me find out this device of satan, I used to say to the latter, when he suggested to me that I was ruining my health, that my death was of no consequence; when he suggested rest, I replied that I did not want rest, but the Cross. His other suggestions I treated in the same way. I saw clearly that in most things, though I was really very sickly, it was either a temptation of satan, or a weakness on my part. *My health has been much better since I have ceased to look after my ease and comforts.*"

" There is a false self," said the Dean of St. Paul's recently,† " which must be mortified and crucified before we can attain to our true being. This is in a sense common Christian teaching, though too often forgotten and neglected in an age which has mistaken comfort for civilisation, and which shrinks from bearing and inflicting pain with a morbid sensitiveness."

†Lectures on Mysticism.

True and False Mysticism   In these days of occult research and of a passionate craving for " mystical experiences " of various kinds by which it is claimed that a deeper knowledge of spiritual truth can be gained, it may be well to remind ourselves that there is a false and morbid mysticism as well as a true and healthy one, and that the Fathers and spiritual writers of the Church have always carefully distinguished between the two. As the distinguishing *marks* of these two forms they give the following :

True :

1. Distrust of self. A fear of self-deception which increases in proportion to the increase of grace.

2. Complete submission of the will to God's will and to the guidance of the director.

3. A care to avoid the extraordinary and to conceal it from others when it presents itself unbidden.

4. Great sensitiveness of conscience, a spirit of penitence and a love of mortification.

5. A deep soul-peace even under suffering and when misunderstood and persecuted.

False :

1. A good opinion of self and an obstinate adherence to one's own judgment.
2. An effort to draw attention to oneself; to let others know what grace one is receiving and to arouse their interest.
3. A satisfaction in hearing others speak of one.
4. Sadness at and dislike of humiliation.
5. A craving for consolations in prayer and in intercourse with God, with the cessation of which the desire for prayer also ceases;—a certain sentimental satisfaction sought after in religious exercises and devotions.
6. Restlessness, taedium vitae and a complaining spirit after apparently extraordinary manifestations of grace.
7. A love of the extraordinary and uncommon.
8. Subjectivism and a refusal to submit to authority. The latter especially is a sign that the soul is dominated by the spirit of pride which is hostile to God, even though it may be able to speak of graces lifting it to the third heaven. To this demon of pride the unclean spirit joins himself."

LXII.

From what has thus far been said it will be seen that the Church's teaching respecting these matters is an altogether consistent one. It is based upon the plain words of Christ, as they are recorded in the Sacred Scriptures, upon the teaching of the Apostles and earliest Fathers and Doctors of the Church, and upon facts carefully observed and studied throughout the centuries. Neither the denials of heretics, nor the findings of rationalising theologians, nor the assertions of scientific men have ever caused her to modify her pronouncements respecting the powers of the unseen world and their activities. And modern science itself is surely amply and increasingly justifying her attitude. I have indicated in my earlier works to what an extent many scientific observers of psychical phenomena are, in their warnings and interpretations, approaching the Church's teaching. It is daily becoming more clear that it is only in its form and method that demonic activity has changed. The activity itself continues unabated, and through the rashness of very imperfectly informed experimenters, it is becoming a grave moral peril to Society. By the practice of the many forms of *mind-passivity* which have been found to be the condition of invoking spirit-phenomena, doors are being opened which give close and perilous access of the spirit-world to the minds and souls of unwary men, in numerous instances leading to the loss of all religious faith and to the mental and moral undoing of the victims.

But Science, so rashly opening these doors, has not yet shown us how they are to be shut. The consequence is that they remain for the most part permanently open. And it is probably to this cause, more than to any other, that we have to ascribe that loss of faith in Supernatural and Historic Christianity which would seem to characterise the thought-movements of our day. It is, in my opinion, not argument and controversy which will restore this faith to the world, but a clear and full recognition of the living forces which have been and are instrumental in destroying it. To what an alarming extent and under what ingenious disguises these forces are at the present moment exercising their activities and influence, in almost all parts of the world, is very imperfectly known to the ordinary observer. And it is significant to note that protests and warnings against these occult practices and against the inferences drawn from the results obtained through them, are beginning to come in from the most unexpected quarters.

LXIII.

A Protestant paper recently printed a very admirable letter contributed by a Protestant Indian Missionary who, on his return to England, found to his amazement that those very cults and philosophies which he had been sent to India to condemn and to counteract were not only flourishing in this country, but were being regarded as teachings superior to and in advance of Christianity. The following are extracts from this striking letter:

" An Indian missionary, as he moves about Great Britain, becomes conscious in some places of the presence of a quasi-philosophical atmosphere that reminds him of the land he has just left. Teaching, in which the dogmas of reincarnation, *karma*, occultism, pantheism,

144

and an unhealthy mysticism find place, seems to have crept into the Christian Church, and is, to some extent, responsible for the paralysis that prevails. The Indian missionary is puzzled to find doctrines openly taught which he was sent forth to condemn. These dogmas appear to have a fascination for certain minds, which refuse to receive concrete evidence as to the baneful effects of such teaching in India. They have robbed the Indian peoples of the sense of individual responsibility, have made possible the system of caste, than which in most of its present-day manifestations no grater evil could fall upon the land, and have degraded India morally and spiritually. Men and women write and talk of the spirituality of India, but it is a spirituality that manifests itself chiefly in a ceremonialism of the most materialistic kind, or in asceticism that seeks the salvation of the individual to the neglect of his fellow-man, or in an occultism that desires a short and easy way into the mysteries of the divine—an occultism that parts company with ethics. If men and women who dabble in Theosophy, Christian Science,

145

Vedantism, Bahiism, and other Eastern cults would but learn how these cults have blocked the path of progress, stopped the true culture of the intellect, encouraged the growth of a whole jungle of tangled superstitions and injurious customs, and degraded the individual, they would hesitate to meddle with what has been demonstrated to be so pernicious and paralysing."

" When one who has spent years in the examination of such teaching, and found how hollow, unsatisfying, and hurtful it is, meets with these experiences, one feels that there is abroad a spirit that does not desire to face the facts as they are in the Churches to-day.

" There is an apparent return to the Gnosticism of the early Christian centuries, with all the unhealthy speculations regarding spiritual existences and short cuts to spiritual knowledge; and, if the Churches do not exercise discipline, this will be followed with disastrous moral consequences. In India there is a saying, " The wheel continues to revolve after it has left the axle." It is true that many who profess an interest in these Eastern cults

146

are admirable persons. They retain for a time their Christian ethics; but when the link that unites them with the source of moral power— Jesus Christ, God and man—is snapped, the moral life will shrivel up, and instead of the happy, trustful spirit that knows all things work together for good to them that love God, there will be resort to crystal gazing, spiritualistic mediums, the palmist, *et hoc genus omne.*

" The cause for alarm and sorrow is the position given to Jesus Christ, with the loss of joyous confidence in God, and the teaching regarding sin, with the lamentable moral laxity that inevitably follows.

" In all these cults much is said about Jesus Christ as Master, Teacher, Mystic, Spiritualist; but He is robbed of His true position—' far above all rule, and authority, and power, and dominion, and every name that is named, not only in this world, but also in that which is to come,' and He is deprived of His essential personality—" in Him dwelleth all the fullness of the Godhead bodily "; and He is no longer " the image of

147

the invisible God, the first-born of all creation ; for in Him were all things created, in the heavens and upon the earth, things visible and things invisible, whether thrones, or dominions, or principalities, or powers; all things have been created through Him, and unto Him ; and He is before all things, and in Him all things consist.''

Jesus Christ is but one among many. True, He has usually the first place; but He has ceased to the followers of these cults to be the Source of grace, the Divine Forgiver, the Saviour of men and women from sin, the Divine Healer of humanity. Rob Jesus Christ of this Divine function, and there is no channel for Divine grace to flow into the human soul; there is no Divine dynamic to create man anew and mould character into the Divine holiness; there is no continual supply of strength to perfect moral and spiritual life, and to enable man to persevere in all good works. The sources of moral and spiritual life, light, and strength are cut off when Jesus Christ is removed from His throne at the Father's right hand.

" Many who give time and thought to these Eastern cults and theosophies doubtless think they are honouring Jesus Christ, but a careful examination of their inner life will reveal that things are not what they were. They have lost the joyful confidence in God they once possessed, and have but vague and indefinite aspirations after some impersonal being. The state of mind that exults, ' If God be for us, who can be against us ?' and ' All things work together for good to them that love God,' is as wide as the poles asunder from that which asks, ' Is the Universe friendly ?' Instead of the glad assurance of God's favour in Jesus Christ there is a restless yearning for some spiritual phenomenon or occult mystery. The clear, joyous Christian atmosphere has been exchanged for the murky sky and depressing climate of a spurious spiritualism. Instead of filial access to God through Jesus Christ there is resort to crystal gazing, the mutterings of a medium, or some other occult manifestations. Instead of a healthy, vigorous, individualistic

149

vitality, eager to do, dare, or suffer for God, there is a moral paralysis, a spiritual decay, a deadening fatalism.

" The abandonment of Jesus Christ as Lord, and the acceptance of pantheism, lead to a wholly dangerous doctrine of sin. Members of these Eastern cults try to eliminate this word from their vocabulary, or eviscerate it of its content. There is no place for sin— rebellion against God—in pantheism; to describe men, parts of the Divine, as sinners is a libel; and though in Great Britain men and women may hesitate to say, when they lie or deceive, ' It is not I that so act, but God,' yet the pantheism professed must lead them logically to say as do their fellow-believers in India. When sin is ignored the downward path is easy. The relations between the sexes become lax, integrity is at a discount, manhood declines, and the vague and vapid sentimentalism of a subtle pantheism produces a morbid selfishness and a moral inertia destructive of all true ethical and spiritual vitality."

LXIV.

In his work, "Satanism and Magic" (with a Preface by the late M. Huysman), M. Jules Bois, an experienced student of this subject, declares that

> "a number of persons, not specially distinguished from the rest of the world, are devoted in secret to the operations of black magic, communicate or seek to communicate with spirits of darkness—for the attainment of ambition, the accomplishment of revenge, the satisfaction of their passion, or some other form of ill-doing."

LXV.

In conclusion it but remains for me to point *The one Remedy.* out what neither scientific experimenters nor spiritists and occultists as yet recognise, namely, that increasing numbers of their disillusioned victims are turning to the Catholic Church for healing and deliverance. A kind of instinct would seem to be guiding them in this course. Many of them have previously passed through the hands of nerve-specialists and hypnotists, of

151

healers and magnetisers, and of mediums and other occult operators of various kinds. They invariably found that their last state was infinitely worse than their first. None of these agencies had it in their power to close that mystic door of theirs which they had so rashly and thoughtlessly opened by their experiments. It is in the ordinances of the Catholic Church alone that they are discovering an effectual means of paralysing and shutting out from their souls those dangerous powers of darkness which have succeeded in invading them—in many instances saving them from suicide and the mad-house. They are coming to recognise the fact that the Catholic Church alone possesses the true key to the solution of the psychic mystery.

May we not then reasonably conclude that in proportion as the modern world comes to a knowledge of the true aim and character of these dangerous forces destroying its very life, and as the Church more boldly and vigorously applies the remedies entrusted to her keeping, will the fatal spirit-delusion of these latter days vanish away and will the thinking world once more return to its allegiance to the divine Christ, recognising the deep significance of those weighty words:

" . . . if I, by the Spirit of God, cast out devils then is the Kingdom of God come upon you."

Some Soul Safe-Guards.

I.

NO COMPROMISE.

Experience teaches that man's spiritual enemies inflict most injury upon the soul by working upon natural temperament and disposition. Their work is stealthy and subtle—so subtle indeed that their presence and operation behind the scenes of life are not even suspected. Difficulties, experienced in the spiritual life, are thus apt to be attributed to purely natural causes. And the primary cause may, of course, be a natural one. By nature and temperament we are all apt to be sluggish and indolent with regard to the affairs of the soul. But where this natural tendency becomes very pronounced and no real effort is made to resist it, a door is opened for the evil spirit to enter in, and he enters in and takes possession without the victims being aware of it. He gets it on the current of the thoughts and ideas which

normally pervade the mind and he directs that
current by the most cunning devices.

Now one of the most common of human weak-
nesses is *the tendency to compromise in matters
of religion.*

There is, in the first place, an innate tendency
to compromise in the matter of dogmatic belief.
Few of us suspect this tendency and are on our
guard against it. We are persuaded that we are
quite sound in the Faith. We are fully convinced that we believe all the truths which the
Church proposes for our belief. We would be
offended if anybody suggested that we doubted
any one of them or that we experienced intellectual difficulties.

But we are daily breathing the atmosphere of
non-Catholic thought which is charged with
intellectual questioning or doubt. We are more
or less in touch with the agnostic literature of
our time, and a suggestion here or there, a
flippant remark of some scientific man, is
deposited in the subconscious store-house of our
minds. We do not consciously accept it, it is
true; but we cannot quite cast it out. It connects

155

itself with other similar statements which we have heard from time to time. And, after a while, a hidden doubt comes creeping into the mind. It distresses the mind. It agitates the soul. It suggests all sorts of possibilities. Can the Church really give an answer to the difficulty suggested? Can such and such an article of faith be held, in view of our most recent knowledge? Can an intellectual man really give his full assent to this or that teaching?

Thus the hostile virus works in the mind, and imperceptibly pervades the mind's energy and operation. In the truly Catholic mind it does not perhaps destroy faith: but it paralyses the active operations of faith. It tends to keep the mind in suspense, hovering between affirmation and negation, not doubting any article of faith, but not quite fully embracing and believing it either. The mind, in the attempt to escape the difficulty, vaguely seeks refuge in some kind of compromise.

The process is the same in the spiritual life. Theoretically we all know what our duties as Christians are. We know that if we do not

156

energize ourselves, loyally corresponding with grace and liberally using the Sacraments, we cannot save our souls.

We hold this firmly and maintain it in our intercourse with our fellows. And we have, respecting these necessary duties, the best possible intention. But here again nature constantly tends towards compromise. We have no intention to abandon our position—to neglect our duty : but we are slow in fulfilling it. The noisy world with its thousand interests and engagements surrounds us. It seems happy and prosperous without fulfilling any spiritual obligations. It looks upon them as a waste of time, as an engaging of the mind with matters which are unprofitable and of which one can know so little. It has a hundred practical and plausible reasons to give us why we should enjoy the present, make the best of the life that now is and not waste our time upon that which is to be. It holds before us " a practical, sensible, common sense view of life."

And it requires an effort to go to early Mass, to make a daily meditation, to fulfil the obligation respecting the Sacrament of Penance. Is it really necessary to be so very strict about these matters? Will it not suffice if we avoid mortal sin?

Here again the conflict ends in compromise. Spiritual duties are not neglected, but they are fulfilled with slackness and half-heartedness and at long intervals. The soul's attitude becomes one of hesitation, of a halting between two opinions, of a being neither hot nor cold. Who does not know this condition of soul, and has not striven against it?

Now it is upon this natural human tendency that the evil spirits work. It is this condition of compromise which they endeavour to confirm and maintain, and by means of which they most successfully attain their end. It is to their inspiration that the apparent plausibility of the reasonings of the mind are most frequently due. Theirs is a kind of cowardly underground operation. They are far too cunning to cause an active doubt in the mind and consequent rejection of some article of the Faith. In the Catholic mind this would create alarm. The

158

result might be a consultation with the priest and a good Confession. The intruder might thus be detected and a more vigorous spiritual life might be the result. He would thus be over-shooting the mark, and he is far too cunning to do this. His aim is reached much more effectually by keeping the soul in a state of suspense and paralysis, by reducing all the spiritual activities to a minimum. It is the compromise which gives him the victory, because compromise in these matters ultimately means the sickness and crippling of the soul.

This, to my mind, is the devil's most success-ful work in the modern age. It is not so much loss of faith which the Church is mourning in our day, as a dangerous indifference, a kind of lethargy, a fatal enervating compromise between the claims of the world and the lawful claims of God upon the soul.

In no evil of our time can the hand of the enemy of mankind be more clearly seen than in this one.

We must consequently be on our guard against this natural tendency, and check and counteract it by vigorous remedies in its most initial stages. We must face the fact that the enemy is present, and we must use all the means at our disposal to outwit him.

I would venture to suggest three safeguards, which I and others whom I have tried to help have found useful and effectual.

1. *Avoid desultory and indiscriminate reading.* It is the greatest hindrance to a healthy spiritual growth. We do not eat all sorts of food. We select the kinds of food which we know to be pure and nourishing and which go to build up our physical constitution. We know from experience that some sorts of food, pleasant and palatable though they be, cause sickness and disorder when they are assimilated. If we have any sense we resist the temptation of eating them when they are offered to us.

It is precisely the same with our intellectual food. It is astonishing what an amount of unwholesome and indigestible stuff of this kind the modern man is made to absorb. It is presented to him in the most attractive and palatable forms. Thousands of books are every

160

year issuing from the secular press in which the poison is distributed in the most subtle way and is called by the most pleasing-sounding names.

With every kind of weapon and by the most diverse and artful methods the truths of our holy Religion are attacked. Arguments are used which to the uninitiated and inexperienced seem almost unanswerable. The particular truth itself is not necessarily denied, but, by a subtle suggestion, a new interpretation, a more " rational " mode of presenting it, its hold upon the mind is loosened and faith is disturbed. The forbidden fruit is sweet to the natural mind, and consequently the tendency is to read on, even though the presence of the soul-destroying virus be suspected. The voice of conscience seldom fails to give the alarm; the difficulty is to obey it promptly.

The Church has issued solemn warnings on this point, and her warnings are based upon a long and varied experience and an intimate knowledge of human nature.

OUR DUTY IS TO OBEY PROMPTLY AND WITHOUT HESITATION. We must first of all use discrimi-

161

11

nation in the *choice* of our literature—examine and consider before we open and read a particular book or article. If we inadvertently come upon anything manifestly hostile to our faith we must at once close the book and cast it aside.

This may at first sight appear a cowardly mode of procedure for an educated man; but it is nevertheless a necessary one in view of the peculiar constitution of our nature.

Modern psychology has thrown much light upon our mental processes. We may read a particular statement and attach little importance to it at the time. We may think that we shall forget it before long. But, as a matter of fact, nothing that we read or have read in the course of our lives is ever wiped out from the tablets of our minds. The subconscious store-house has received it and retains it, and some day, by the association of ideas, worked upon by evil spirits, it will emerge from the store-house; it will present itself in a still more attractive dress, and it will trouble and torture the mind and even tend to destroy faith. In no sphere of her manifold activities has the Catholic Church shown so clearly the watchfulness of a mother's care as in that of our literature. Unceasingly and with all earnestness she warns her children against bad books clothed in attractive form, and against indiscriminate reading. Such reading is the curse of our age and the source of numerous moral and spiritual evils.

To such as are attracted by the sceptical religious literature of our time and who imagine that an educated Catholic, if he would move with the times, must know what non-Catholic thinkers are saying and writing, I would say:

The Church has been on the scenes for nearly two thousand years, and she has witnessed many transformations of thought. She has stood unmoved. What objection can a modern man raise against the faith which has not been raised some time or other and which her theologians have not met fully and effectually?

Have not the best minds, in every age, and the holiest of men given their unhesitating assent to the truths of faith and found nothing in them that could be regarded as contrary to enlightened reason?

163

Is it not as true in our own as in our Lord's day that " the sensual man perceiveth not these things that are of the spirit God ?"*

Is it not true that God is apt to hide His mysteries " from the wise and prudent and to reveal them to little ones ?"†

Therefore just as you keep out of your body poisonous and indigestible substances, so keep out of your mind and soul poisonous and soul-destroying ideas. The evil spirits will then find nothing in your mind upon which they can work, and with which they can connect their promptings and suggestions.

2. *Correspond instantly with the faintest movements of grace.* We have to bear in mind that if evil spirits are, in accordance with the divine plan, permitted to assault and tempt us, opposing influences are incessantly at work. We are never tempted beyond our power of endurance. Our Guardian Angel is near. Our Lady and the Saints are ever interceding. The grace of God, by the movements of conscience, or direct inspirations, is waiting to visit the

*I. Cor. ii., 14.
†St. Matthew xi., 25.

soul. It is but necessary that the will should energize itself in the right direction and, by a deliberate choice, seek and embrace the higher good. But the choice has to be made. We are not automatons. God will not save us against our wills; with fear and trembling we are to work out our salvation*. A Heaven which is forced upon us could not be Heaven under any circumstances. We must choose and desire and strive for Heaven if we are to enjoy it. But the tendencies of our fallen nature are downwards; they are flesh and world-wards. We are surrounded by the powers of darkness and fascinated by things that allure and captivate the senses. And these are apt to close tightly the door by which alone grace can enter in. The evil spirits make it their business to *keep* that door closed.

But in all human lives there are moments when the door opens: some unusual event of life, disturbing its normal current; loss, trouble, suffering of mind or body; perhaps a warning uttered in a sermon, a good Confession or Communion, and possibly, on the other hand, a

*Philip. ii., 12.

165

sin-stricken conscience. The mystic door opens and, for a brief moment, God speaks. It is the hour of grace in the day of His visitation. The evil spirit will suggest a natural cause; He will counsel caution and delay; the danger of nerve-excitement. Our Guardian Angel will urge obedience and submission and prompt action, so that the tiny spark of grace may be fanned into a flame. At such moments hesitation and compromise are dangerous things. We must obey at once, and without reserve, because the voice of grace may not speak again for some time. In some instances it may never speak again. "Circumstances" may prevent it. Death may occur. Life is short. In any case in another moment the influences of the sense-world will re-assert themselves and they will re-absorb the interests and activities of the soul How often, for instance, is some mysterious influence, at quite an unexpected moment, gently but earnestly urging us to prayer. All the circumstances are favourable for entering into vital relationship with God, for deepening our soul's union with Him. It is a fatal thing to allow such opportunities to pass and to let so-called

166

"practical reasons" to influence the will. So much may depend upon that moment. God, it is true, may speak again: but the circumstances may never again be quite the same; the soul never again equally well disposed. In the spiritual life too, as in all great crises of life, we must act promptly and with decision. Let us remember our Lord's words: "If thou also hadst known and that in this thy day the things that are to thy peace, but now they are hidden from thy eyes."*

3. *It is well to make a frequent and emphatic Confession of Faith.* And it is well to make it in an audible voice. This tends to rouse the soul from its lethargy, breaking in upon that dreamy and hesitating state of the mind which is so fatal to the spiritual life. It is a bold breaking through the barrier which the evil spirit is seeking to erect. It is a tearing of the net in which he is striving to entangle the soul.

Such a confession of faith is apt to scatter the clouds and mists which have gathered round the spirit, and if the doubts and difficulties be real and persistent, let the cry be: Lord, I believe;

*St. Luke xix., 42.

167

help Thou mine unbelief. It takes the mind away from the thoughts and impression in which it has begun to habitually engage and acts as a kind of suggestion and stimulus. One part of our mental being is made to take a decisive step as it were, and the other part which has been lagging behind assents and begins to follow. A certain warmth and confidence is spread over the soul, and its higher faculties are awakened and called into operation. Such a simple but open confession of Faith, in the form of the Creed for instance, or the simple act of Faith in God is thus often the crisis in the indisposition of the soul, ultimately resulting in convalescence and recovery. The evil spirits, in any case, recede from such a soul with haste.

II.
GUARD YOUR SENSES.

We are beings of a composite nature, made up of body and soul. And although these are, in a certain sense, quite distinct from each other, they are nevertheless intimately joined together, one acting upon the other, one strongly affecting and influencing the other. The sense-impressions naturally are the more powerful ones of the two because the material world from which they emanate surrounds us, and we cannot, under any circumstances, escape from it even if we would. We cannot get out of our bodies. It is in our bodies and by means of our bodies that our spiritual education is carried on.

The workings of grace, on the other hand, reaching us from the invisible spiritual world, are, generally speaking, vague and faint. They come and go, sometimes when we least expect them, and unless we make strenuous efforts to retain them by cultivating a certain condition of receptivity and " by curbing all our senses under discipline," they but lightly touch our soul's life. In any case, under ordinary circumstances, the sense-impressions are far more vivid and imperative, and the probability is that their effect and influence can never be entirely wiped out. Here, too, our human nature exhibits the wound and flaw which it has received by reason of the fall. There is a disorder, a want of harmony in it, the origin of which nothing else in the world can explain.

Theologians teach (and experience confirms this) that while the evil spirits cannot *directly* influence the inner citadel of the soul, they can and do effect this by means of the senses. They can act upon the senses and vivify the impressions which these convey. The consequence is that if we want to safeguard our souls we must watch over our sense-life. Theoretically we know this; practically we ignore and deny it. We carelessly allow the soul to be flooded with a very world of unwholesome pictures and ideas, and then we wonder why we make so little progress in the spiritual life—why our intercourse with God is so cold and halting.

Take, for instance, the sense of hearing. What damage does it not inflict upon the soul if it be not carefully guarded and watched over? What poisonous and unwholesome stuff is not reaching the soul's centres by this one channel in the course of a single day? We know the evil thing from its effects. " As often as I have been amongst men," writes Thomas à Kempis, " I have returned less a man." We know what the writer means. We have experienced this sense of nausea and self-contempt if we have ever taken ourselves seriously. It is the protest of the immortal soul against injury which has been inflicted upon it by indulging in or listening to debasing and unprofitable conversation. We have come away from such conversation with our spiritual perceptions blurred and injured, annoyed with ourselves and with those who have exposed us to the injury. We have found ourselves unable to pray and to entertain a single elevating thought. We have resolved, in a vague and undefined sort of way, not to expose ourselves unecessarily to such perils. We are anxious not to be suspected of fanaticism and of narrow-mindedness. We do not care to appear eccentric and peculiar. And besides this, there is a side of our nature for which the light and frivolous talk of superficial and frivolous men and women has a peculiar fascination. Criticism of the character and doings of our fellows, of their possible motives, condemnation of them, if possible, is gratifying to our vanity. It puts our own imaginary virtues into a clearer light, and makes us hug ourselves in our self-righteousness.

There is a similar attraction in questionable plays and songs; we like them even though we inwardly condemn them; we return to them as the moth returns to the light of the candle even though it has badly burnt its wings.

It can serve no purpose to deny all this. The full recognition of an evil is the first step towards effectually correcting it. Half-cures, based upon an imperfect diagnosis, are of no use whatever in these matters. All sensible men know that things are as I have stated them. But what very few realise is the fact that by these apparently trivial means grave and permanent injury is infallibly inflicted upon the soul.

And this is true for more reasons than one. The human mind, in its subconscious activities, is a very delicate and impressionable thing. Every intelligible sound which reaches it from the sense-world is permanently recorded. It is there transformed into ideas and conceptions of the most complex character. After a while these penetrate into the conscious working mind and take their revenge upon the life and character of those who have allowed them entrance. But, worse than this! *the evil spirits avail themselves of the material which they thus find ready for their use.* Their action becomes that of the photographer who develops the sensitive plate upon which the invisible impression has been formed. And they do more than this. They enlarge the picture. They bring out a variety of shadows and details and astonish the mind by ultimately presenting the picture in a form which the mind quite fails to recognise as its own.

Thus it comes to pass that many a passionate craving, many an unlawful desire, terminating in a mis-directed life, strong aversion to prayer and spiritual exercises, actual and wilful neglect of spiritual obligations may often be traced back to some light and frivolous remark listened to in a conversation, to some flippant suggestion, quite innocent perhaps and permissible in itself, but charged with disastrous consequences to the soul's life.

A correspondent writes to me :—

" An eminent Dublin specialist told me of the case of a Carmelite nun, melancholia, I think it was, who used filthy language. He made inquiries, and found that when she was

173

a child she lived in a house in London behind which were some mews and where she must have heard the language used which was quite foreign to any of her other surroundings. . . Now why out of all possible echoes should she have given these? They were special London obscenities whose meaning could not have been grasped."*

" It is certainly a curious thing from the purely scientific point of view, that in so many mental cases the language should be blas- phemous and obscene when the subject is ordinarily pious."

The process, of course, is the same with respect to the sense of sight. The eyes have been rightly called the windows of the soul. Few people have any idea how much injury is inflicted upon the soul by the unguarded use of this faculty and to what extent the powers of darkness avail themselves of the door which is thus carelessly opened. It seems such an innocent thing to stop at a shop window and to gaze at an unclean picture calculated to play

* Some priests in New Zealand told me of a similar case.

174

upon the sensual part of our nature. It is almost impossible in our days to avoid doing this. The thing may have happened before we have realised it. And our better nature may assert itself, and we may pass on our way after a while, even mentally condemning what we have seen. But if we have lingered at all the mischief is done. The photograph has been taken. The image has been formed in the mind. It may lie there undeveloped and forgotten. But the day invariably comes when some temptation will assail the sense-life, when the imagination will be set to work. The picture will then be developed, the image will rise from its subconscious store-house and will form the background upon which the temptation will construct itself. It will take the particular shape which the material, lying latent in the mind, will cause it to take.

This work beyond all doubt is the work of the demon. We cannot, in reason, imagine that any part of a man who in any sense desires to live a godly life, can act in such hostile fashion towards another part. Besides this the pictures formed are often painted in colours which are

175

quite strange and out of keeping with anything the mind, by its natural disposition, is ever likely to form.

A long experience in connection with abnormal psychical phenomena has convinced me that we are here on the demon's track.   I have come in contact with men, earnest and sensible and well-meaning men, who have vainly striven for years to shake off one such a haunting impression or image, formed perhaps under circumstances which they could scarcely control, but in the course of time distorted by the demon out of all proportion and into a never-ceasing torture and temptation.

The safeguard is simple and suggests itself. The difficulty is to keep it in mind and to employ it rigorously and on all occasions. We must strictly guard our senses, and, so far as unwholesome impressions are concerned, we must tightly close those doors against them which lead to the citadel of the soul. We must take care not to furnish the devil with fuel for the fire which he is striving to kindle.

We must make up our minds to cut and avoid places and persons through whom injury is thus likely to be inflicted upon our souls. This is really a much easier thing to do than one is apt to imagine at first sight. It requires a little courage and determination—a casting aside of the fear of man and contempt of his sneer and ridicule. We must cut out for ourselves a distinctive path through life and, in this respect, ruthlessly push aside every person who threatens to obstruct it. The prize is well worth the effort. What matters it, after all, if flippant and indifferent men and women who recognise no higher duty or aim in life think us strange and eccentric? St. Bernard says: " One cannot be perfect without being singular." And St. Alphonsus adds: " If we would imitate the common run of men, we should always remain imperfect, as for the most part they are.' We are, alas! living in times when the man who allows his mind to become a kind of cesspool, a receptacle of all sorts of impurity is regarded as the sensible practical man of the world, while he who seeks to sanctify himself is looked upon as abnormal and peculiar. But we may be sure that matters look very different from God's point of view. Christ declares that " the clean of heart shall see God,"* and the Apostle spoke of " holiness without which no man shall see God."†

III.

LEARN TO BE ALONE.

" With a distracted attention," wrote Fr. Hecker, " the soul can never attain to perfect union with God."§

One might enlarge this thought and say: With a distracted attention it is not even possible to pray well or to attempt any kind of spiritual life.

And one of the many causes of a distracted attention, beyond doubt, is the craving for society—the aversion to being alone. So great indeed and universal is this aversion that it may be regarded as a characteristic failing of the modern man, which is largely due to the conditions of our modern superficial life, but to some extent too to our own fault. I have

*St. Matthew v., 8.
†Hebr. xii., 14.
§*Questions of the Soul.*

personally known men and women who had become so utterly the slaves of this weakness that they had fully persuaded themselves that they would go mad if they had to be habitually alone.

So far as the world at large is concerned it is not difficult to analyse the causes which lie at the root of the intense craving for society. It is not always due, as is generally believed, to the love of pleasure and the desire of being entertained. Sense-pleasures of every kind, the rush to dinners and parties and even to meetings and lectures, when nothing better can be had, produce taedium and disgust—they lose their attraction after a time. We know this from the atmosphere of weariness and satiety which emanates from worldly men and women. The deeper-lying cause is probably the fear of being alone—the vague desire to get away from thoughts and reflections which cause distress and uneasiness. However plausible our philosophy of life may be, the voice of conscience, pointing to graver duties and responsibilities, will somehow make itself heard and the most convenient way of silencing it is to seek company. There is, in intercourse with our fellows, a certain sense of security, a feeling of safety produced by the consciousness, that however unsatisfactory our life may be, it is at least shared by so many amiable and well-disposed persons.

Unhappily the spiritual man cannot altogether free himself from the influence created by the modern conditions of life. There are certain social duties to be performed, and it is for some a most difficult thing to secure retirement. Indeed so great is this difficulty in some instances that retreat to a religious house is the only condition under which it can be secured. The benefits thus apt to be gained prove perhaps most conclusively what an immense amount of good might be gained from diligently cultivating the *habit* of being much alone.

In any case the fact remains that the soul cannot expand and grow, and that the voice of God cannot make itself heard when a hundred jarring voices are all the day long buzzing around it. They cause dissipation and distraction and make that growing self-knowledge and union with God upon which the spiritual life depends almost impossible. A further difficulty, of course, is that while the cultivation of social duties and relations comes easy to us, the education of our spiritual nature demands effort and self-denial and calls for the presence of a living and active faith.

Now I am firmly convinced that the enemy of mankind works upon this innate weakness of our nature, and thus gains his unique victories over the soul. Consider how clearly, in our best and holiest moments, we realise our duty in this respect and make fervent resolutions, and how frequently and effectually we are apt to be thwarted. We attribute this thwarting to " circumstances " over which we persuade ourselves that we have no control, but how often does the real cause lie in ourselves? There is before every spiritual mind the ideal of a nobler spiritual achievement—of a closer and more intimate union with Christ. And subconsciously there is the full intention to enter upon this higher course *some* time. But, the demon argues: there are pressing duties to-day, and therefore the matter must be put off till to-morrow—better still, till next week. The circumstances will then be more favourable. There will be more time for prayer—more leisure for meditation and for effectually attending to the affairs of the soul. And there is about these suggested hindrances such an air of reasonableness and plausibility that the more practical side of our nature is quite satisfied and assents. And yet there is perhaps all the while an underground sort of feeling that we are deceiving ourselves, and that the thing could be done if we were really determined, if spiritual duties and interest engaged our attention in the same degree in which social and temporal duties engage them.

Thus, by these simple tricks of suggestion, adapted to our natural temperament, does the demon forge our soul-fetters and maintain the distance which separates us from God. For who is better acquainted than he with that innate weakness of our nature which, while recognising the spiritual law, is nevertheless unwilling to obey it, and to which St. Paul gives such emphatic utterance when he says:

182

" For I am delighted with the law of God according to the inward man: But I see another law in my members fighting against the law of my mind and captivating me in the law of sin that is in my members."*

Here too, therefore, it is well to be on our guard. We must not attribute too much to " circumstances." We must at least suspect the source from which the " circumstances " arise, and thus outwit the devil if he is concerned with them. The disastrous effects of many of the modern conditions of life, entailing constant superficial intercourse with others, can be observed even in the natural order. It destroys all originality of mind and of character. It paralyses the very power of independent thought and reflection. People who are never alone live in other people's ideas and absorb and then reproduce their thoughts. Their very souls cannot be said to be their own. Fact and truth have little weight with them. They often repeat parrot-like what some person, more distinguished for social position perhaps than for wisdom, may have said or may be known to hold

*Romans vii., 22, 23.

about a certain matter, and a modern drawing room is thus often a veritable parrot-house—a place where a very world of intellectual energy is being dissipated.

But greater by far, of course, is the injury thus inflicted upon the spiritual side of our nature. Its best energies and noblest possibilities are frittered away, and, after a while a kind of lethargy creeps over the soul. The spiritual world recedes from the mind in proportion as the mind loses that power of retiring into itself which can best, perhaps only, be cultivated by isolation and separation from the great multitude.

It is here surely that we must seek for the true cause of that " loss of the sense of the Supernatural " which the Catholic Church is so deeply bewailing in our time.

" The desires of sense," say the " Imitation," " draw thee to walk abroad; but when the hour is past, what dost thou bring back, save a weight upon thy conscience and dissipation of heart?"

" God and the holy angels will draw nigh to him who withdraws himself from his acquaintances and friends."

184

It is surely well for us to remember one thing. However much and long we may have found it possible to find diversion and satisfaction in social intercourse, whatever degree of comfort and fancied security the society of friends and relations may have brought us, we must die alone, quite alone.

The hour must come when, alone and separated from our fellows, we must pass into the Unseen—to the judgment seat of God. Is it not more than probable that we shall then regret keenly that we have not cultivated the habits of being much alone with God while in the body, and that as a consequence we have to appear before Him with our energies dissipated and our souls in confusion and disorder?

IV.
NO UNLAWFUL MENTAL PASSIVITY.

There is a certain receptivity of mind which is intimately connected with the spiritual life and upon which it may be said to depend. It is that lawful passive attitude towards God and the supernatural order by means of which the obstacles which hinder the action of the Holy Ghost upon the soul are removed and the grace of God accomplishes its work. In the spiritual life, in any sort of intimate relation between the soul and God, it is always necessarily a matter of co-operation. God warns and admonishes and invites; the uplifted Christ draws the heart*; the Holy Ghost convinces of sin, of justice and of judgment†. But every Christian knows that these divine operations are by no means compelling. We may experience their full force, and yet we may resist them. We may be in active conflict with them for years. God impels, but He does not compel. The will remains free, and we are left to make our choice. And it may continue *permanently* in opposition unless we cultivate a certain passive attitude towards God, unless we open wide the doors of our hearts for His grace to enter in.

But this submission to God, this opening of the door of our higher nature, is no weakly, sentimental attitude of the mind, dependent perhaps upon temperament; it is a very definite

*St. John xii., 32.
†St. John xiv., 8.

186

operation of the will. It is co-operation of the human will with God's will. It is the persistent and constant determination to be a learner in the school of Christ and to receive as a free gift from God what He alone is able to give. It is the effort to resist the influences which are at work in our hearts and in the world tending to prevent us from learning our lesson. There is involved in this idea the notion of energy and determination, not of dreamy, sentimental imbecility. " Be *subject* to God," writes the Apostle St. James, " but *resist* the devil, and he will fly from you."

Indeed, considering the tendencies of our nature, there is perhaps no operation of the soul which calls for a more decided and constant exercise of the will. The apparent paradox, therefore, is quite intelligible. Just as we have to be weak in order to be powerful†, so we have to *will* hard in order to be receptive or *submissive* towards God.

There is, however, another kind of receptivity or mental passivity of which we hear and read a

*Ch. iv., 7.
†II. Cor. xii., 10.

great deal at the present time and which is often confounded with the attitude of mind and will of which I have spoken. It is a sort of caricature or travesty of it—a morbid and unwholesome state of mind and body induced by unlawful and dangerous occult practices. The devil, as many of the saints tell us, is the ape of God, and there is little in the supernatural order which he does not strive to copy and imitate. And in some instances these imitations are so successfully planned and carried out that even the cautious and wary are apt to be led astray. The extraordinary success of the various occult systems of our day affords ample illustration of this truth. The devil's track can be discerned in most of them. They all claim to be but a better and fuller development of some Christian idea or to tend to a more vigorous exercise of some Christian practice, yet they all ultimately lead to the rejection of essential Christianity. Their devotees invariably fall victims to a wholly pagan and unchristian cult. In most instances the error is not detected until the gravest possible mischief has been done. I could, from documents in my possession, write many pages on this subject illustrating the truth of my statement. But I have already treated the matter at full lengh in several of my books.*

There is, of course, all the difference in the world between the lawful attitude of mind demanded by Christ and that counterfeited by the demon. There is a difference both in respect of nature as well as of effect.

The first attitude is, as we have seen, a normal and healthy state of mind and soul. It is produced by the will disposed by grace to take up a diffident, submissive and receptive attitude towards God. It is a state in which *our consciousness remains intact,* and in which the highest and noblest powers of our nature are called into operation. Even in its very fullest development, in the states of ecstasy with which we are made acquainted in the lives of the saints, no injury is inflicted upon the bodily or the moral nature.

The second and unlawful condition is the complete surrender of the will, terminating in the *loss of consciousness* and calling into activity the lower forces of our nature, stimulat-

*See *Modern Spiritism; The Supreme Problem.*

ing the sense-life and the passions. It is the surrender of reason and of self-control, terminating in physical and moral helplessness.

The effect of the first condition is joy and peace of mind, a growing love of Christ and His law and a desire to enter into closer communion with Him. It is a hatred of sin and a constant and burning desire to conform the will to Christ's will and to bring the understanding into captivity* to submit to the persons and ordinances which Christ has ordained and instituted. *It is the shutting of the door which gives access to the evil spirits.*

The effect of the second condition is distress and mental disorder—an indescribable restlessness of mind. It is aversion to prayer and real spiritual communion, to the Sacraments and observances of the Church—often deliberate hostility to the person of Christ. It is a state of nerve-weakness or neurasthenia, not infrequently leading to organic disorder and mental aberration. It is a state of imbecility and helplessness *facilitating the invasion of evil spirits.* To put it briefly, therefore, while the first condition is

*II. Cor. x., 5.

190

that state or attitude which opens the door to the Holy Spirit of God; the other attitude is one which throws it open to the invasion of spirits, of created beings who, as all experience proves, are in most instances the enemies of man as well as of God.

We must, therefore, guard against *all forms of unlawful mental passivity*, against the use of any kind of devotion or practice which is not fully approved of and sanctioned by the Church. We must be suspicious of all kinds of private devotions respecting which she has not pronounced judgment. The times are evil, and Satan transforms himself into an angel of light. The most attractive and plausible-sounding invitation in this respect may conceal the poisonous shaft. Those promulgating these things may not themselves be aware of what they are doing. The demon, in our time, be it remembered, does not appear with horn and hoof; he is far too crafty to pursue so clumsy a policy. He adapts himself to the tendencies of the times and plays the part of the prompter who controls the situation, but who is well hidden from sight. His trump-card is to create an impression in the world and in the minds of clever men that he does not exist, that such a notion is irrational and unscientific. And while they are disputing amongst themselves as to the probable origin of much that is so mysterious in nature and in the life and mind of man, he successfully carries on his warfare and wins his battles. His presence and activity may be inferred from the incontrovertible fact that the ultimate effect of all these occult systems of thought and practices is the separation of the soul from the Supernatural Order and its re-absorption into paganism, in whatever attractive and plausible form that paganism may present itself.

In a recent letter from a thoughtful correspondent there occurs the following passage:

" A feature which has impressed me when reading of spiritistic experiences, etc., is the *psychic passivity* involved in all these varieties of substitutes for Religion. Not merely with mediums, but with Christian Scientists, New-Thoughts folk, New Buddhists, etc., there is that practical feature of false mysticism present. . . . In all there is some process employed whereby the higher powers of the soul, the intelligence and the will, are brought into a passive or lethargic state. It is curious how this ' quietism ' runs through so many types of religious error. It is the attempt of the soul to seat herself in the highest place and has the general result of being sent down to the lowest place, i.e., being deprived of the natural exercise of her natural freedom and made the plaything of demons or of her own lower appetites.''

I can but point to the actual facts of experience of which there is such abundant record in our days in confirmation of the truth of these statements, and I would urge the reader to weigh these matters well in his own mind.

INDEX.

INDEX.—(Continued.)

INDEX.—(Continued.)